UASE URBAN ACTION SHOWCASE & EXPO

10th Anniversary Celebration - Times Square
November 4th & 5th 2022

The Urban Action Showcase & Expo 10th Anniversary Celebration exploded on Times Square with the pioneers of Martial Arts and Action Cinema.

Friday November 4th ignited the UASE 10 celebration with a gathering of celebrity guests, Industry professionals, sponsors and a select group of fans at AMC Empire 25 Theaters on 42nd street in the heart of Times Square. The evening brought together many of the inaugural Action Icons that launched UASE 1 for a Red Carpet Reception and Awards presentations. The Dragons: Taimak aka Bruce Leroy from the iconic cult classic The Last Dragon, Michael Jai White The Black Dragon (Black Dynamite, Spawn, Triple Threat), Ron Van Clief The Black Dragon (The Black Dragon, The Black Dragon's Revenge), and Don The Dragon Wilson (Blood Fist, Black Belt, Ring of Fire)

lit up the Red Carpet. They were joined by Action Cinema pioneers Fred The Hammer Williamson (Black Caesar, That Man Bolt, Three the Hard Way), and Grandmaster Carl Scott (Kung Fu Executioner, Soul Bros of Kung Fu) as well as Action stars Robert Samuels (The Gambling Ghost, Made in Chinatown), Vincent Lyn (Operation Condor, Tiger Cage), Hakim The Machine Alston (WMAC Masters, Mortal Kombat), R. Marcos Taylor (Straight Outta Compton, Baby Driver) and Amy Johnston (Accident Man, Lady Bloodfight).

Immediately following the Red Carpet Reception, all guests convened inside of the Theater for the Urban Action Showcase International Action Film Festival (UASIAFF) Awards which include The Behind the Action and Diversity in Action Awards presentations. DJ Winn set the tone with classic R&B Top 40 hits as guests took their seats. The atmosphere was charged with excitement, love, respect and camaraderie as familiar faces embraced again for the first time since the Pandemic.

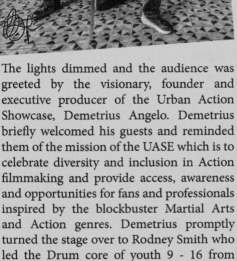

The lights dimmed and the audience was greeted by the visionary, founder and executive producer of the Urban Action Showcase, Demetrius Angelo. Demetrius briefly welcomed his guests and reminded them of the mission of the UASE which is to celebrate diversity and inclusion in Action filmmaking and provide access, awareness and opportunities for fans and professionals inspired by the blockbuster Martial Arts and Action genres. Demetrius promptly turned the stage over to Rodney Smith who led the Drum core of youth 9 - 16 from

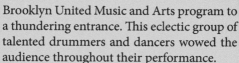

Brooklyn United Music and Arts program to a thundering entrance. This eclectic group of talented drummers and dancers wowed the audience throughout their performance.

The UASIAFF has officially begun as promotional trailers from sponsors and guests entertained the crowd. Demetrius returned to the stage to honor his staff followed by an Alumni Appreciation Awards presentation for the Day 1 celebrity guests which included Ron Van Clief, Taimak, Michael Jai White, Fred Williamson, Don Wilson, Warrington Hudlin, Ric Meyers, Robert Samuels, Vincent Lyn, Willie Johnson, Tayari Casel and Art School Dropouts.

Stunt Performer Calif Guzman was the recipient of the Behind the Action Award for his accomplishments in Stunts. Amy Johnston was the recipient of The Phoenix Award which acknowledges Action Stars on the rise. Amy was honored for her roles in Accident Man, Lady Bloodfight and Stunt Performance in Black Widow.

Two more amazing performances took place between the presentations. The crowd got to experience the mindblowing Matrix like performance of Robin Channing who bent, twisted and melted metal spoons with only his mind before our astounded audience. The crowd also was treated to an awe inspiring performance by Wu Fam during our Jim Kelly Tribute! All of these performances can be found under the UASC TV tab on UrbanActionShowcase.com

The night concluded with the Urban Action Showcase International Action Film Festival Awards honoring filmmakers from around the globe. All UASIAFF 2022 Winners can be found on UrbanActionShowcase.com under the UASIAFF tab. The Margaritaville Resort Hotel Rooftop Lounge hosted the honorees and guests for an evening of celebration to cap off Day 1 of the UASE 10th Anniversary.

Day 2 of the UASE 10th Anniversary celebration brought out the Fans, Martial Arts Masters, Cosplayers, Celebrities, Family and Friends to a day of Pop Culture Exhibits, Panels, Seminars and Festival Screenings. The UASE screened over 40 hours of independent and mainstream content that included the celebration of iconic Martial Arts and Action cinema presentations of Blade 2, Equilibrium, and The Transporter 20th Anniversaries, along with Super Cop 30th Anniversary. A special screening of Game of Death Redux wowed the audience and was followed by a Q & A with producer Alan Canvan and Moderators Ricky Baker and Ric Meyers.

Unique Action Cinema Seminars such as Willie Bam Johnson's Call 2 Action Martial

©DozenFingersPhotography

Arts Action Talent initiative, Hanshi Nikwan Murphy's Fire Arms 4 Film, The Woman King introduction to Bladed Weapons with Lady Sensei Gerry Chisom, LightSaber training with Rogue One and How to Shoot Fight Scenes on an Iphone with JFH all took place on the roof deck overlooking Times Square with unprecedented sunny 75 degree F weather. You couldn't ask for better conditions for a 10th Anniversary celebration!

The UASE is often described as a Family Reunion with all of the family members that you love! The UASE Love fest continued

throughout the day with Celebrity Fan Photo and Autograph sessions, Interviews, Cosplay, VR and Virtual Photo Experiences where fans were able to interact with nostalgic content like Mario, Fortnite, Teenage Mutant Ninja Turtles, The Last Dragon, Wakanda, Mortal Kombat, Resident Evil, The Matrix, Crouching Tiger Hidden Dragon and more!

The evening came to a close with more UASIAFF screenings and the Deadly Art of Survival Honoree Awards. Fans capped off the evening with another amazing night at The Margaritaville Resort RoofTop Lounge.

Overall UASE 10 was everything and more than anyone could ask for in a 10 year celebration. The atmosphere of love, honor and respect embraced everyone in the room and all you could see was joy everywhere that you looked. We are truly grateful to all of the Fans, Family, Friends, Icons and Sponsors who have made the UASE what it is today.

When doing a multifaceted event like the UASE you just try to remain focused so that all of the events are executed well. You don't really think about anything else so each year you just keep climbing. Like the steps in a

4

staircase, you continue climbing until you reach the desired floor. We haven't reached that floor yet so we are still climbing. We hope to continue the legacy of 5 star service and entertainment focused on celebrating diversity and the multicultural achievements in the blockbuster genre for years to come.

Written by Demetrius Angelo (Founder and Executive Producer of the UASE multi platformed movement. Sponsored by the HBO Cinemax brand)

Films Anniversary Screenings and Fan Experiences

The event's schedule was as follows:

10th Anniversary
1. Avengers (Virtual Fan Experience)
2. The Dark Knight Arises (Virtual Fan Experience)

20th Anniversary
1. Equilibrium (Gun Kata Virtual Fan Experience)
2. Resident Evil (Virtual Fan Experience)
3. Blade 2 (Screening)
4. The Transporter (Screening)

30th Anniversary
1. Passenger 57 (Screening)
2. Super Cop (Screening)
3. Rapid Fire (Screening)
4. Universal Soldier (Virtual Fan Experience)

40th Anniversary
One Down Two to Go (Screening)
Blade Runner (Virtual Fan Experience)

Spot Light Screenings:
Game of Death Redux
Flatbush Fists
Sons of Newark
Urban Action Showcase International
Action Film Festival Official Selections

Stars, past and present, memories

Amy Johnston
Urban Action Showcase and Expo is an event like no other. It is highly entertaining with some of the finest performers and

also incredibly insightful, inspiring and educational with panels from top professionals.

I personally think UASE is a great opportunity for young filmmakers, upcoming actors, stunt professionals, and more to show their work through the award ceremony to industry professionals as well as mingle with them throughout. I was so honoured to join the 10th anniversary and it felt like I became a part of the family as it's a very personable event.

I highly recommend any lovers of martial arts, films, TV, and overall entertainment to join this awesome event. You won't be disappointed! Most importantly Demetrius is absolutely wonderful and the best host! Did I mention it's in one of the best cities in the world? NYC!

Don't miss UASE!

Carl Scott
Mr. Demetrius Angelo, the brilliant CEO of UASE, invited me to participate in the Urban Action Showcase experience. I had the honor of being present with legends such as Lady Sensei, Master Ron Van Clief, and Robert Samuel. In addition, I had the opportunity to interact with Michael Jai White and Fred the Hammer Williams. There was a genuine outpouring of love for martial arts among all those who attended this event.

Cynthia Rothrock
Since its inception, the UASE has been one of my favourite events. In fact, over the

for what I call "our martial arts family." Anyone who is a martial arts enthusiast and who wants to excel in the art of film will immediately be bound together with a shared passion.

I also love how women are highlighted and elevated for their success and contributions to the world of martial arts.

This event is for everyone, from the most seasoned film industry professionals, actors, directors, and producers to the new martial arts students interested in improving their skills and techniques. You will learn, see, and experience much at this wonderful venue. You're also guaranteed to make new friends and connections to last a lifetime.

The UASE is an event that cannot be missed!

Jose Manual

The Urban Action Showcase is a great platform for people of colour and minorities to express and empower their talents. My first visit was in 2015 and ever since I've been following it every time I get a chance to attend I do and since I am usually working on an action project I submit.

years, I've only missed attending one due to filming a movie. This event ranks as one of the best and classiest-run events to honour filmmakers and martial artists. New York City's prestigious location makes it a perfect place to attend to enjoy the city and its historical sights and city lights.

What I love most about this event is that new actors and directors get honoured, and

I always meet and make new friends in the industry. I always enjoy watching the films presented and conducting seminars to help martial artists who want to get more involved in the film industry. I've found attendees with great potential to excel in both the film industry and martial arts.

The event's atmosphere fills with a love

BAN ACTION SHOWCASE AND EXPO
10TH ANNIVERSARY
URBAN ACTION SHOWCASE
FILM FESTIVAL 2022
UASE 10TH YEAR ANNIVERSARY
WARNER BROS. DISCOVERY
ultimate wireless

Its just great friends in a positive wholesome environment celebrating action pictures and martial arts, its a great place to be for a guy like me who dwells in action movies all the time.

The festival doesn't just limit itself to minorities but I know it is the hook for them if you want to rephrase it like newcomers or new action talent feel free to do so.

The Urban Action Showcase gave me a forum and a great community to share my passion and I've been really grateful for that. This year I showcased my short film "Boriken: The land of the Brave Lord". It was fun meeting you guys.

Lady Sensei – Chisom Gerry

The Women's Martial Arts Network has been proud to be a sponsor and friend of the Urban Action Showcase and Expo; we were overjoyed to help celebrate the 10th

Anniversary in Times Square.

It was a wonderful and bittersweet reunion and a much-needed renewal. In the three years since the pandemic, we lost so many of our comrades. We gathered to remember and recall them. We also saw familiar faces, and celebrities and made new friends along the way. It was good to see so many people come out to celebrate.

Those of us in the martial arts took lots of group photos together with Photographer Erskine Isaac, attendees took photos with some of their favorite action heroes and sheroes like Fred Williamson, Ron Van Clief, Taimak Guerrero, Michael Jai and Gillian White, Robert Samuels, Don Wilson, Vincent Lyn and soooo many others. Cosplay was alive with people dressed as their favorite action sheroes and heroes. It was a very spirited celebration.

Although I have personally supported the UASE since 2016, the Women's Network

has been a sponsor for the last five years because of Shihan Demetrius' commitment to diversity and multiculturalism. The UASE presents very strong and prominent platforms for women that align with our mission, which is "Our Images...Our Voices and Our Stories...Can Inspire the Next Generation" We really believe in the positive images of female sheroes and defenders, martial arts practitioners and action movie stars. It was an honor to host the "She Reigns: Sheroes of Action Cinema" panel discussion.

The audience was fascinated to hear and learn about the industry from my special guests, stunt performers Amy Johnston (Lady Bloodfight, Female Fight Squad) Evelyn O. Vaccaro (Black Panther 2, John Wick 3) and Valisa Tate (Journal For Jordan, F.B.I. Most Wanted) The day was uncharacteristically warm for November; we did our workshops and seminars outside on the rooftop of the AMC Theater overlooking 42nd St. With the release of The Woman King, it was a timely honor and opportunity to teach a workshop

I wish they would bring in some different people along with there regulars.

Robert Jefferson
To call The 10th Annual Urban Action Showcase a "great event" would be a nondescript compliment that lacks any nuance necessary to accurately describe the experience.

It was great. But that is almost beside the point. Perhaps, because of where I am in life, or where I am within the life of the event itself; I found myself standing around in certain moments & allowing myself to soak up the vibe with hope of perhaps gleaning a tiny amount of intellectual understanding of how such a thing even exists.

I've attended at probably every level, participant, competitor, award winner, and, most recently, showcase artist. As awkward a platypus as I am, it dawned on me that I've never truly felt out of place here. Perhaps it's the warm, inclusive vibe of it all that makes this event truly special. Every smile, hug & handshake reminding me of the extended family fellowship with here each time I come.

utilizing circular movement, recreating some of the blade work fight sequences used by Viola Davis and the Agojee characters.

Attitudes are really changing because this is the first time that so many men and young boys easily joined the workshop with the women. Ordinarily, my workshops are attended by all women, but this year we broke some barriers so that was such a pleasant and timely surprise. I'm really excited for the exponential growth of UASE and we look forward to another stellar year, we're already in the planning stages to expand with other women's groups in 2023, so we're pretty excited.

Perhaps it's something more ephemeral. In any case, all the laurels gained by our two films, (Jugando Con Fuego & Shadow Fist 2 respectively) didn't quite provide the sense of satisfaction enjoyed in the experience of screening our films for the UASE audience. That they were enjoyed by all meant even more.

I thank my brother Demetrius Angelo for all the blood, sweat, tears, and love poured into this stellar event, and look forward to the next 10 years of Urban Action.

Robert Samuels
I remember the first time being invited to the HBO/CINEMAX sponsored URBAN ACTION SHOWCASE...The energy was simply palpable. So many of my heroes in attendance. That being said every year the event just continues to become bigger and better …

I have continued to support Demetrius Angelo and his dedicated staff because they are doing something that has never been done before providing a platform of inclusion and uplifting people of color and the next generation of filmmakers.

Michael Woods
For me it was a good experience I went I think for two years I got to meet a lot of people on the industry that I heard of but never meet because I stay to my self I found the panels informative for people interested in breaking into movies or just to learn about it also they got to meet some of the movie actors.

I think it would be great for people to check it out also there are some real martial artist there it's in a great location my only gripe is

Demetrius has create a way for everyone to have an opportunity to network and grow as filmmakers so many films submitted and recognized from across the globe. I am apart of the executive board of advisers along with Warrington Hudlin. This year was our 10th anniversary!!!

Who would have ever thought that we would reach this milestone. When I look at year one when we offered so many opportunities to young upstarts in the business...10 years later some of those same individuals and now household names in the film community. That would not have happened if not for Demetrius Angelo and his vision of giving recognition of the past, present, and future stars of tomorrow....hopefully we will have this same conversation in another 10 years.

Robert Bobby Samuels H.K.S.A

Rochelle Miller

It is a fact that acting, stunt work and filmmaking opportunities are not as plentiful for minorities. This holds especially true here in the United States. As an African American woman and consumer I have personally witnessed an innate lack of diversity in the films and other programming in my demographic. To put it bluntly, representation deeply matters, and it matters on all levels of visual entertainment.

For those who have broken these often impenetrable barriers; celebrating debuts, release date anniversaries and other milestones, has become the UASE method of showing the world that we want more! More diverse leading roles, and more culturally based or independent filmmakers sponsored from script to screen. To fill this void, the UASE has -unilaterally and relatively overnight- become the "necessary" we didn't know we needed.

That said I am so unbelievably proud to have

been a part of its platform (while wearing many hats in the interim) over the past 10 years."

Vincent Lyn
I have attended the Urban Action Showcase Expo from the very first event to the recent 10th Anniversary that was held at the AMC Theatre in Times Square.

I have to first give kudos to the organizer HBO Producer Demetrius Angelo. Many people don't realize what it takes to put on an event of this magnitude.

There are so many pieces to the event that need to be put in place, and not to talk about all the artists, talent, and background help, attendees and of course sometimes certain egos that are assembled under one roof. It takes a lot of careful planning and time, so if not for Demetrius's vision and the ability to adapt to the change in the entertainment industry in the past ten years. There would be no event and certainly not lasted as long as it has. That in of itself is an incredible achievement.

For many of my generation of peers it is also wonderful to reunite and enjoy some quality time as we know full well there are some friends who have passed on to the next life. So, we share a common bond of camaraderie and this event has been a wonderful place to all call home. We are all so busy with our own schedules that a year will go by without

seeing each other. For just that one reason it is extremely special to me. As long as I'm around living and breathing I will always make my best effort to support the Urban Action Showcase Year. See you next year. Peace and blessings

Willie "The Bam" Johnson

I would just like to say this event continues to satisfy Mr. Demetrius's commitment to excellence and humility to the fans in the legacy of This genre of films.

We have been working together for the last 10 years with our collaboration for what we call call to action martial arts talent Showcase. And we have provided me up at unities for people that are truly successful in the film industry today and many of today's great heroes of action films I've been judges

and mentors to the talent.

The thing is still out this year for me personally was Fred "The Hammer" Williamson taking the time to talk with my son Marshieh Johnson About his career in education. Messiah the honour roll student and champion Black Belt along with the star of the award winning film 1 out of 100 along with the new comedy short 34 chambers.

It was his desire to be involved in football now Mr Williamson spent well over 30 minutes and guiding him and giving him advice on how to follow his path in Gobion. He is truly a hero of my generation and the next generation, what an honour.

https://www.williethebamjohnson.com/
https://filmfreeway.com/1OutOf100

SUGAR CAYNE .COM

SUGAR CAYNE .COM

Taimak

The Glow behind 'The Last Dragon'

By Simon Pritchard

Taimak Guarriello (Known as "Taimak", pronounced Tie - Mock) was born on 27th June 1964. Taimak's father is an originally from American Naples, Italy. His mother, an African-American, was from Harlem and was the first person to open a Soul Food restaurant in Chelsea, London called "Laurita's". Taimak is an actor, stuntman, and martial artist; best known for his leading role in the film "The Last Dragon".

Taimak has gone on to be a trainer, and martial arts choreographer, starring in TV shows, working on music videos, opened a gym, released a fitness DVD, starring in a hit Off-Broadway show - Roadhouse The Comedy, and much more…

SP: What was it like growing up in New York?

Tai: My father was a Singer, my mother was more or less, well, used to work at the Apollo as a young kid and she was married before my father. She was married to a very charismatic amateur boxer, a golden glove champion and also a Harlem gangster, They met when she was 17 and he was 18 years of age in Harlem. Long story short, he went to prison for robbery and not too soon after is when she met my father.

They were part of a very, what is it? Bohemian, a very popular group of artists. Just imagine The Apollo in the 50s and 60s.

James Brown was there with my mother and people like, Andy Warhol, Jackie Wilson, Jimi Hendrix the whole scene.

SP: Your family spent a lot of time between New York and London. How was this time?

Tai: We moved to Europe when I was very young, we went back and forth. I lived in London and Rome, Italy mostly. My parents split up in Europe, my father went back to New York and my brother and I came back after. My mother and sisters stayed in

Europe a little while longer. When we came back to New York when I was like 13 or 14, it was the mid-Seventies, the Eighties.

Although very upsetting as a kid, It was still the most extraordinary experience living in Europe with my parent's friends. But also, as I told you before, when we returned to New York City there was a lot of danger, there were no cameras in the streets, no cell phones like there are now, cameras all over New York City. Hard to get away with anything really today. When you walk the streets in the daytime, it was OK, and when it got dark, you better know what corner to turn, and what corner not to turn, when someone's walking towards you, you gotta be ready for anything. The artistic aspect of the Seventies and the Eighties was the best. You had everything from Pascal to Warhol, all the fashion, Austin Blutler, Alexander McQueen came a bit later. There were all these different landscapes, but they had darkness too, so it was like both extremes.

SP: Who, if anyone, were you named after?

Tai: The guy I was named after; my father used to take care of, Teimoc Johnston-Ono. He was about six to seven years old. My father didn't even know he was going to turn out to be a Judo World Champion. When Taimak was born my father wanted to name me after Teimoc, but he didn't remember the spelling of his name. So he spelt my name, T A I M A K, pronounced "Tie-Mock".

My father was in the village a lot, (Downtown manhattan) and he saw a bunch of kids ranging from 7-14. the 7 year old was always dirty, but cute and my father took a liking to him, met his parents and used to take the kid to his mother to clean him up. The kid whom he never saw again when my father moved away with my mother. He left a soft spot in my father's heart...They didn't have the Facebook back then and he lost contact with "Te-imo-c". He didn't know the spelling and named me Taimak.

SP: Bruce Lee was very influential at this time, what was it like?

Tai: Martial arts blew up in the 1970s because of Bruce Lee and when he passed, it stayed alive by aspiring Chinese martial arts actor who tried to replicate Bruce Lee, some were entertaining and talented, some were down right bad, and never met the mark. Everybody and their mother wanted to learn martial arts and everybody had their own idea of what 'that' was. Ultimately it was an exciting time for people.

SP: What martial arts have you studied? What were the martial arts like in the Seventies and Eighties?

Tai: I completed in both full contact Karate (kickboxing) and point Karate. I won in the New York State Championship in kickboxing and I won some Karate championships. One is essentially knockout, one is not knockout which I would compete in for speed and timing mostly.

Then you had a bracket of martial artists at the time that were all kinds of characters. They were very theatrical and came out, some of them even walked the streets with martial arts-looking gear on, it was crazy!

You had people who would come to these tournaments, breaking ice or breaking bricks with their heads, some of these guys within these prologues of movements and breathing techniques performed a monologue!

There was one of them we liked to watch,

he was a huge powerful guy, with a big belly, but he broke all of this ice and even glass like this. He used to call himself "Jeeter the Master Breaker". All these different martial artists, it was an extraordinary time.

SP: What was it like back in the Seventies and Eighties in New York City?

Tai: There was a mass of disco music, so I can't deny that there was a party scene that was exploding at that time. It was an exciting and fun time as a teenager, music playing through boom boxes in apartment buildings as well as tuned to favorite radio stations walking the streets. Even if you didn't get into clubs, you heard about discos that older adults frequented, from students.

But there were good things and bad things about it because of drugs and all that. So it's good and bad. It was at the start of "House music" scene, but at the beginning they didn't call it House music. It was a mix of R&B and other music. The Grandmasters of the scene were The Paradise Garage's home dj Larry Levan and others like Frankie Knuckles, Nicky Siano, Kenny Carpenter (Studio 54), David Mancuso, François Kevorkian, there were others all amazing.

SP: How did you keep your life on the straight and narrow considering all those bad influences around?

Tai: My father was kind of ol'skool tough. but at the same time, I loved my father deeply. As his son you knew that you had to

stay away from certain things. I knew that when things went too far, either there were guys that were too violent or they were too strung out on drugs.

When a young person has one or two parents, hopefully healthy parents. it's great to have a healthy balance as a parent, install love, but with a balance of a little fear and respect. So they get out there on their own, they're thinking about what the consequences will be, not only health-wise but in many ways.

My mother's best friend at the time, Curtis, tells the story of his mother who raised him, when he was a teenager and he tried cocaine and accidentally he left a little bit inside of this box in his room. His mother would go clean his room and she saw what was inside the box pointed at him and said "Come here, come here". He came over and she slapped the shit out of him.

He said, "What's going on!?" She then pointed at the powder, "What is This?", he said some lie and she said, "No it's not, it's cocaine!" And then he was a wise guy and said to her "Well, how do you know?", there's always a consequence.

SP: From training in Karate which is a strong form. How do you find the transition into Chinese styles? How did you pick it up?

Tai: I was always good with adapting physically, because I loved martial arts so much, I had the passion to learn and I still do. So i had relax more.

Growing up in NYC doing martial arts and competing it was always about how strong or how fast, you were and how much endurance you had. I wanted to do more of the external stuff that looks amazing in movies. I really didn't delve into soft style until I got injured eleven years ago. So because of the injuries in my spine, I was locked up. It was quite shocking.

That's when I started understanding what they mean by soft style. It's a whole other thing. like when you look at the ocean. Bruce Lee talked a lot about it. Be like water. That's what soft style is. Chi is electricity one can generate within themselves. Imagine electricity entering water, it's a whole other thing, it's the healing part, breaking down and building up. You need to know the hard and the soft.

SP: What do you think between technique and power?

Tai: Yeah, you get to a certain level physically, and you're training with certain cats that are highly skilled, Olympic athletes, Judo and so on. Judo requires a lot of focus, because you can get thrown on your head or ass in a blink of an eye, it's definitely necessary to have good technique. If you just have technique with no strength, the technique is meaningless, you must understand the soft and hard.

SP: There are many stories about how you got the role in "The Last Dragon", how did it actually happen?

Tai: I won the New York State Kickboxing championship in 1983, but that was when I was eighteen. I was contemplating going to college and studying some kind of physical therapy, but everybody in the martial arts community said that there was a film, and they were looking for a person of colour to play the lead. Everybody was saying that I should go up for it.
Funny thing was everybody was going up for it, from all races, White, Black, Latino, and Asian for example. I eventually got an audition. I wasn't an actor. I didn't know anything about the process and I thought it was going to be a karate demonstration, some kind of Kata, but Cast Director, Jeremy Ritzer was there at the time who I was dealing with. He gave me a peice of the script (the sides) and I saw other people outside the office with

papers in their hands. When I went into the room, eventually, I did horrible!.

No acting experience. He said "You look the part, but you just gotta work on that"

I was upset because I got my hopes up. My father called me a few days later. He knew I was talking about this because everybody got me hyped up that I'd do well. He said. "Look, we're gonna go down to Miami. Tell your friend Richard to come with us". Richard was my best friend at the time.

While we drove down to Miami, my father said "Hey, I can tell you're still pissed about that audition, you know I had some acting experience so let me help you". My father was kind of tough guy and I didn't want to go through it with him. My friend was sitting in the middle of all this, I was sitting on the passenger side and my father was driving. Long story short, he kinda pushed me along to do the scene I read at the audition and when I didn't do right he'd whack me in the back of my head, "Hey! Come on!, you don't know what the hell this is about?" And I was like, "no!", I was litterally like "Bruce Leroy" in a way. Anyway, when we got there I immediately got out of the van, I was pissed with my father and didn't want to have anything to do with the role and I wanted to let it go completely.
My friend came over to me and said "if there was a God on Earth, that role was written for you", and something inside me told me that was true.

Me and my friend had a lot of fun down there in Miami while my father was working. my friend and I cleaned roofs to make money and go out to the beach and coconut grove, a great hang out spot back then. While we cleaned the roofs, we had fun going over lines from the movie.

By the time we got back to New York a couple of months later, I heard they already hired someone for the role. I wanted to go back to the casting office and give it another shot anyway.

I went down there, knocked on the door and they said "Look Well, we already hired somebody else". I said, "Please let me at least read once. I pleaded with him, he let me in his office, really he was just trying to get rid of me. But after about 10 seconds into reading the scene, he was blown away by my reading. He quickly stopped me and called the production office. The guy that was chosen for the role hadn't yet signed the contract so they fired him and hired me. So there you go.

SP: "The Last Dragon" brought in at the box office three times the budget and is considered a cult classic. Were there any plans for a sequel?

Tai: Many plans! plans plans plans... Without getting into all the details. it was just never the right time. It wasn't in the stars. Unfortunately for so many people that love "The Last Dragon" and want to see a continuation.
It's been so many years anything is possible, you know, but I don't want to get into it yet.

SP: What was it like trying to learn to act whilst on set?

Tai: Everyone is an actor and I always felt I had a nature for acting. The thing was, to carry a whole film on your shoulders without being in any movie before, it is not easy. My martial arts experience, my work ethic and my discipline were really high. The good thing was they got a acting coach, Richard Fancy and Michael Schultz's wife, there to support me.
The thing was, when I showed up to the very first shoot, they asked me to step in front of the camera. As soon as the camera was focused on me, I really felt at home. I felt a sense of knowingness, a sense of peace. Like, "I can do this". So. that sense was important for a young talent to have confidence and then they'd help me through the tough times.

SP: "The Last Dragon" is a wild ride that is about a martial arts student and a fan of Bruce who embarks on a spiritual journey to unlock the power of 'The Glow'. What are your best memories this film?

Tai: Getting the film was like a shock. All my childhood I wanted to be a superhero because I dealt with being bullied as a child. I was always walking around with a cloud

around my head. So. I was like, Wow! I was nineteen and they said they want you to play the star of a major motion picture, a super hero!
You're nobody and you're not even an actor and you're the star of the show. That's the stuff you dream about.

SP: Yeah, that must be unreal!

Tai: Yeah, imagine an unknown, a non-actor and then being chosen to play James Bond.
When I got to the set it was like walking into your favorite comic book it was over the top. Everybody was focused because they were really excited to be part of it, you know? And it had Michael Schultz at the helm as a director and Berry Gordy looking over things. You had all these talented people behind the camera. Joseph M. Caracciolo,Production Manager, smaller roles played by William H Macy and Chazz Palmetieri.
Doing a film it's not just the talent, it's everybody else running around making sure it's all running well.

SP: What did you do throughout the rest of the 1980s and 1990s?

Tai: I was teaching, boxing, kickboxing, did stunt work, some fight choreography, I was modelling; I was really hustling. I was doing commercials, and regional theatre when I was in L.A., modelling I was making sometimes $1,500 a shoot, catologue work paid well, which was great. But then there was this emptiness because of not getting acting roles.
So all this stuff, choreography, commercials, modelling, was just to be able to pay the bills really. It didn't happen until I started to get a sense of how to manage my money and how to make things happen.

The Comic-Con route was great because fans were able to meet me in person and buy some personally autographed photos, that's been going on for a long time now. The Comic Cons are getting big in Europe and I haven't done any there yet, I'd love to. Actors have to find a way to keep creative, keep a roof over their shoulders and keep food on the table at the same time. Some wait tables, but I think it is so important for an actor to find a financial balance to free them up. Also to have a business strategy.

SP: You had success as a choreographer and what was it like working with artists such as Madonna and Gwen Stefani? What was that like?

WHO'S THE MASTER?

BERRY GORDY'S
THE LAST DRAGON

SUN DUM GOY

TRISTAR PICTURES PRESENTS "BERRY GORDYS THE LAST DRAGON" A MOTOWN PRODUCTIONS PICTURE
Starring TAIMAK JULIUS J. CARRY III CHRIS MURNEY LEO O'BRIEN FAITH PRINCE GLEN EATON and VANITY
Director of Photography JAMES A. CONTNER Executive Producer BERRY GORDY Written by LOUIS VENOSTA
Produced by RUPERT HITZIG Directed by MICHAEL SCHULTZ

PG-13 PARENTS STRONGLY CAUTIONED
SOME MATERIAL MAY BE INAPPROPRIATE FOR CHILDREN UNDER 13
ORIGINAL SOUNDTRACK ALBUM AVAILABLE ON MOTOWN RECORDS AND CASSETTES
DOLBY STEREO IN SELECTED THEATRES
A TRISTAR RELEASE 1985 TriStar Pictures All Rights Reserved.

Tai: Yeah, yeah. Gavin Rosedale (I was introduced to him to choreograph his next video) was dating Gwen Stefani and he wanted me to do some sessions with her because she wanted to get in shape. I choreographed his music video and I also wore a Samurai outfit, in Bush's music video "The Chemicals Between Us". https://www.youtube.com/watch?v=9AtnKPh-hE8

I also did the martial arts choreography for Madonna's "Sky Fits Heaven" number *https://www.youtube.com/watch?v=sU9vpNNBjg0*

SP: As well as music you have guest-starred on several television shows, including "Ally McBeal", "Beverly Hill 90210" and "Third Watch", to name a few...

Tai: Yeah, I did some shows like "Different World". I am talking to my agent about a one-man show in New York. We're looking into that.

Right now I'm starring in a reoccurring role in a show and it's the fifth season coming. The fourth season aired in February 2023 and it's called Double Cross. Double Cross is not martial arts, it's a drama, a thriller. It's about sex trafficking, but it's like a Hollywood version of sex trafficking. During the shoot I was recovering from a bad spinal injury. I didn't feel or look myself.

I play a pivotal role there and I'm in four of the episodes so far. This is the first time I have had a reoccurring role in a tv show. It's on Amazon Prime now and on the All-Black Network.

SP: How did you get into the UFC and officiate in matches in UFC 6 and UFC 7?

Tai: It was when Ron Van Clief became the Commissioner, they were looking for referees and they asked if I would do it so I did it for a little while. It was interesting because back in those days you had no weight class and you had these guys that were wanna be WWE wrestlers. They were very animated just because the producers at the time, were more about exploiting the fighters and making it a big wild circus type thing.

I refereed a fight where the guy had fangs in his teeth...

It was a pivotal time when in those days if you don't know how to get beyond a good striker you were going to get knocked out. However, If you don't know how to get up from the ground and someone is good at grappling, you'll get choked out. If you know wrestling, sambo or Ju-Jitsu if it's done correctly, one can nullify punches and kicks, if not oh boy watch out.

When Dana White took over, they wanted to make it more of a professional athletic organization and they wanted to develop relationships with the fighters that were long term. Rather than short-term.

SP: How do you think UFC has come over time compared to traditional martial arts?

Tai: One of my best friends moved to Florida; he's not a martial artist, but he thinks he can have conversations with me about fighting and martial arts because he watches the UFC more religiously than me. I do like watching it because I was studying Ju-Jitsu before I got injured with Marcelo Garcia where I got my purple belt, so I got to study the grappling skills.

I really liked watching the different techniques on the ground from Ju-Jitsu to Sambo and the shifts to Kabib and Islam Makhachev, the Dagestani style of grappling which is really high level, then you have the Ju-Jitsu competitors that work off their back, you get the Wrestlers working top position and then it's how strikers are able to navigate all that. I find a lot of holes with some of the strikers, but fighters have to be tough to get it in there, you gotta have a heart of courage.. It is the technique and the conditioning which has become more high level where you can't any longer just have a great grappler or great striker; they need to know the full spectrum.

SP: You also performed in the wrestling organisation "Ring of Honour", which has merged into AEW (All Elite Wrestling), alongside Jimmy Wang. How did you find the wrestling industry?

Tai: Well, it's different. It's like learning a different martial art because it's is choreographed… sometimes:). Jimmy Wang was a fan of "The Last Dragon" and happened to walk into a fitness studio I had back in the day and wanted me to do some pro-wrestling with him.. I said yeah sure, b I said yeah sure, bu… sounded intriguing, but I don't know anything about WWE wrestling, I just had amateur wrestling experience in high school.

So he took me to this camp for about a week. It taught me how to fall wrestling style and different moves, how to act it out, with and heels in the faces.

It was pretty hilarious and I had this move I did, where I stepped on the guy's thigh and throw a kick over his head and back kicked him with the same leg and everyone loved it. I respect the wrestlers and the relentless work they put into it. It's definitely a craft.

SP: You have achieved so much, what are you most proud of in your career so far?

When I was just going through all the different highs and lows, the tough times, just to be able to do a short film of my own years ago was rewarding, bring other actors together. To develop something just to be able to accomplish things on my own without Hollywood was like a big deal for

me..

But now I'm ready to go back and work in Hollywood, I could and might write a book on how to deal with all the bs.

You could do some things in Hollywood. And still, if they don't want you to work, you won't work.

There are a lot of politics and a lot of sharks in Hollywood.

Obviously the #MeToo movement opened up a lot of the ugly side. There are a lot of

TAIMAK
THE LAST DRAGON

AN AUTOBIOGRAPHY

wonderful people in Hollywood though and when you find them don't let them go, I didn't really know how to navigate that before.

So my problem was, just as a person getting through all that and still have my health. A lot of people end up OD'ing on drugs or end up completely broke or worse sell their souls, some are in prison. So, I went through some very difficult times.

I really had to chose what I wanted to do with my life.

The fans so powerfully and in my corner, they wanna see me out there, that was one of the things that gave me the impetus to keep fighting. I thought if these people are still out there, and enjoy my work and I love the craft, I gotta stay in. I didn't think it would turn out to be decades later but everybody's got a different journey.

SP: What are your plans for the future and is there anything you are currently working on you can tell us about?

Tai: Yeah, like I said about that one-man show but that's too early to talk about. I'm talking to legendary director Michael Schultz, that directed "The Last Dragon" and so many others. There's a lot happening but best not to talk about it too early on.

My appearances are on my Instagram page @ iamtaimak and TheLastDragon. bigcartel.com. That's the best way to find out what's happening, and because I post everything there, whether it's acting or appearances. I was in the March 2023 edition of "The Deadly Art of Survival" here in New York signing the magazine cover. there will be other appearances coming up that I'll post on my page.

SP: Thank you for speaking with us and it's been an honour.

African-American, was from Harlem and was the first person to open a Soul Food restaurant in Chelsea, London called "Laurita's". Taimak is an actor, stuntman, and martial artist; best known for his leading role in the film "The Last Dragon".

Taimak has gone on to be a trainer, and martial arts choreographer, starring in TV shows, working on music videos, opened a gym, released a fitness DVD, starring in a hit Off-Broadway show - Roadhouse The Comedy, and much more…

Teamed up to tear them up.

The new action adventure fun picture of the year.

HoT PoTATO

Plus The greatest martial arts movie of all time.

Enter The Dragon

A WEINTRAUB-HELLER PRODUCTION · JIM KELLY · GEORGE MEMMOLI in "HOT POTATO" Starring GEOFFREY BINNEY · IRENE TSU and JUDITH BROWN as Leslie
Produced by FRED WEINTRAUB and PAUL HELLER · Written and directed by OSCAR WILLIAMS
From Warner Bros ⓦ A Warner Communications Company [PG] PARENTAL GUIDANCE SUGGESTED ⬦
SOME MATERIAL MAY NOT BE SUITABLE FOR PRE-TEENAGERS

BRUCE LEE · JOHN SAXON · AHNA CAPRI in "ENTER THE DRAGON"
Co-Starring BOB WALL · SHIH KIEN and Introducing JIM KELLY Music: Lalo Schifrin
Written by Michael Allin · Produced by Fred Weintraub and Paul Heller in association with Raymond Chow
Directed by Robert Clouse · PANAVISION® · TECHNICOLOR® From Warner Bros
[R] RESTRICTED Under 17 requires accompanying Parent or Adult Guardian ORIGINAL SOUND TRACK ALBUM ON WARNER BROS RECORDS A Warner Communications Company

22

BREAKING BARRIERS

"ROBERT SAMUELS' Martial Arts Mastery" By Simon Pritchard

SHADOW FIST 3
The final chapter

From Directors Robert Samuels & Robert Jefferson comes an original tale of Martial intrigue

30 years after the events of Shadow Fist a new warrior seeks to find and wield The Immortal Scroll of The Shadow Fist.

This time Sister Moon, a disciple of a venerated lineage of respected masters, along with her brother Lu Chen, is on the hunt. As they travel along to the undisclosed location, the two discuss what it means to be worthy of wielding the item.

Meanwhile, the nefarious Chi Sha Gang has other plans for the scroll. The evil Master Deng wants it for himself and sends his gang to intercept the pair & retrieve it for himself…by any means necessary.

Who will possess the Immortal Scroll of The Shadow Fist? And who is worthy to wield it?

R4FILMS in Association with Champion Spiritworks LLC Presents the Final Chapter in the Action Packed Saga. Starring, Award Winning Mexican Action Actress Roxalinda, Vazquez & Miguel Alexandro Peralta.

BLVCK OUT

From directors Robert Samuels & Robert Jefferson comes a mind-bending tale of action and intrigue.

Viktor is an agent, a special courier who carries biological compounds in his blood, chemicals of a more than questionable nature. We join him for his last, & perhaps, most difficult job to date. Of the 20-plus jobs he's done, this one causes a negative reaction thus sending the whole job into a tailspin of mistaken identity, intrigue & espionage.

Viktor must make the pilgrimage to an undisclosed location in Mexico in a race against the clock. If he fails to meet the timeline, he dies, taking millions along with him. To make matters worse the chemical in his bloodstream causes him to black out and come to after long stretches of fugue-like consciousness. Worse still a group of apocalyptic zealots is hot on his trail trying to cause the unthinkable: the death of untold millions.
Can he make it to his appointed destination, or will the terrorists win?
Who can you trust when the enemy is within?

Robert Samuels
From Enter The Dragon *to my vision*

By Simon Pritchard

SP: What was the first martial arts film you remember?

RS: I remember the first Martial arts film I saw was Five Fingers of Death.

SP: When were you first introduced to Bruce Lee?

RS: The Very first Bruce Lee film I saw was Enter the Dragon. Enter the Dragon holds a special place in my heart now and forever. Once I saw Bruce Lee for the first time, I was in awe of the charismatic man that was in my opinion the fastest Martial Arts that I have ever witnessed on screen. I was so enamoured with Shaw Brothers and Golden Harvest Studios and those films; I wanted to work with those legends.

SP: What stood out about Enter the Dragon that intrigued you then?

RS: Bruce Lee offered me a different look at Martial arts cinema at that time. I remember wanting to be like Bruce Lee. But Enter the Dragon also offered me something else; to see a man that looked like me, Jim Kelly.

He was so cool I remember saying to myself...if he can make it in martial arts films then I know I can. That's when my journey really started to take shape. Now fifty years later, I have had a storied career that has paralleled the aspects of my childhood and dreams of becoming an action actor.

SP: How did that come to fruition?

RS: I went to Hong Kong to pursue my dream of being in action films. With a lot of faith and a lot of luck, I was able to reach certain pinnacles in the Hong Kong Film Industry. I met Sammo Hung and that's where my life changed forever. Living and working with Sammo he would always share personal stories about Bruce and his influence on him as a film-maker. He loved Bruce Lee and was more honoured to have had the opportunity just to work with him. Now thirty years later,...I am a Director.

SP: What were the more practical elements of filmmaking you learned?

RS: One of the things Sammo told me was Bruce was always into creating interesting characters. The biggest influence in my career as a director is I love to create characters that the audience can live vicariously through.

SP: Did you ever meet Jim Kelly?

RS: No, but I admired Jim Kelly just as much as Bruce Lee. I never had the chance to meet Jim Kelly but I was completely shocked and flattered when Jim's family decided to bless me with the first Jim Kelly Lifetime Achievement Award at the Urban Action Showcase. It was one of the most important awards that I've ever received in my lifetime.

SP: IS there any other person that holds a place in your heart from this era?

RS: The other person who holds a special place in my Life is Angela Mao Ying "Auntie " to me. Angela and Sammo are very close and when she found out that I was Sammo's student, she told me to call her "Auntie".

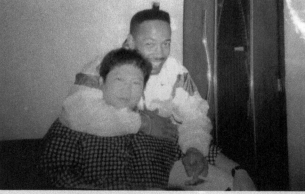

SP: You have two new films coming out, the first Shadow Fist 3; the final instalment to the trilogy. What are people expecting from this?

RS: This time we're focusing on the history of the scroll. We want people to feel the emotional side of the film as well as the martial arts. This was one of the focuses for us. We want this to feel more cinematic for the audience.

SP: "Blackout" seems to be back to the Action-Thriller genre. What made you wish to go back in this direction?

RS: We like to challenge ourselves and Robert Jefferson came up with the concept of a man that believes he's one thing but that's not necessarily the truth. This was a perfect vehicle for me to play a different type of role, along with Roxalinda Vazquez playing a tremendous role and Angel Brophy. In this dark noir, we are showing our range of genres and versatility.

SP: Thank you and we wish you and Mr. Jefferson all the best.

KICKING
BACK IN TIME

The martial arts journey of
Steve Muhammad in
Enter The Dragon
By Rick Baker

Rick: OK, Steve, could you please tell me a little bit about your career and how you got into martial arts?

Steve: Oh, yes, sir. I think I was about 13 years old when I asked my mom if I could go out and get a job, and she said yes. I looked for a job all day and couldn't find one until I saw this Chinese restaurant. I went inside and asked them if I could work with them, and they said yes. Then, they asked me what I could do, and I said I could mop the floors, wash the dishes, and do everything that a young man could do at that time. What I found out two weeks later was that they were teaching a form of karate back in those days, the word "karate" was not so well known.

Rick: Can I just step in there? May I ask in which year this happened, when you discovered martial arts?

Steve: this was around 1956 or 1957,

Rick: long before the Bruce Lee craze in '73, right? This was long before Bruce Lee started influencing people to learn Kung Fu and karate, correct?

Steve: what I was saying. I had never heard the word "karate" before, only the word "judo." Back in those days, there were no karate schools.

Rick: Yeah, same for my father. He did judo during the 1950s. Sometimes, you'd see in the back of comics that offered to teach you by books in jujitsu. They had options like boxing, judo, or jujitsu, Although Karate was available there was very few schools you would have to go to London the word

Kung Fu wasn't really common knowledge until the TV series and Bruce Lee brought it to our attention.

Steve: Yes, sir. So, I practiced Tai Chi for a total of five years. When I graduated from high school, I joined the Marine Corps. They sent me to Okinawa, and there I encountered a guy teaching hand-to-hand combat. While watching, I thought, "I've seen something like this before," which was similar to the Tai Chi I had been practicing. After the training, I approached him and asked if I could show him something similar. When I demonstrated, he said, "Oh, Tai Chi." I responded, "No, this is a Chinese exercise," pretending to know what it was. Coming back to America, I enrolled in Ed Parker's School under my teacher, Daniel Rosado. I studied karate with him until I reached the Brown belt. Then, I saw Chuck Sullivan come into the school and put on a demonstration. Since he and I were about the same size, I asked him if I could transfer from my school to his. He said, "Steve, this is the military. You can come over and join whenever you like." That's where I've been ever since, with kempo.

Rick: Did some people take up martial arts for self-defence? I know Donnie mentioned he took it up to defend himself, and some people pursue it for its discipline or as a form of exercise. What sparked your interest when you first encountered martial arts? Did someone or something grab your attention during your early years, and what were your initial goals with martial arts as a young man?

Steve: Well, during my time in Okinawa, I was fascinated by how they executed kicks and punches, their movements, and how they used their feet much like their hands. This intrigued me, so I began trying to learn what they called "Goju" in Okinawa. However, due to my role in Recon, I had limited time. Most of my time was dedicated to their needs. Still, every three or four months, I managed to spend about a week at the school, training for about two days a week. I did this for a little over a year before returning to the States. When I got back, I joined Chuck Sullivan's school and started training with Danny in the Santo. That's where I established my foundation. I never

the Santo's school, their approach to martial arts, the philosophy of when, where, and how to fight, fascinated me. So, I continued my training and didn't leave until I went to Chuck's school.

Rick: Were you involved in tournament competitions in those days? It seems like you were.

Steve: Yes, that was my aspiration. I wanted to participate in tournaments, even though I lacked sufficient experience. I remember my first tournament. The referee instructed us to bow, and I did so too did my opponent. We assumed our stances, and when the referee said, "begin," my opponent kicked me. I had planned to use a technique called "Five Swords," but I realised too late that he was kicking, not punching, so he earned a point. We continued, and I thought he would punch this time, so I prepared to execute "Five Swords." Yet, he kicked again. As we stood there, the referee declared him the winner on that side. I approached the referee and voiced my confusion. He explained that my opponent had earned two points, and that's why he won. It was a lesson for me that I needed more training.

Rick: It seems sparring in those days was more challenging and less safe compared to today, with all the protective gear. Back then, control over punches and kicks were crucial, wasn't it?

Steve: That is true. It was pretty rough back in those days. You could come out with your teeth knocked out, a black eye, a bloody nose, or a cut on the side of your face. Even with all that, we considered it controlled at that time.

had the opportunity for a solid foundation during my time in Okinawa.

Rick: Did martial arts become a passion for you? Did it consume your life, as it does for some who immerse themselves in it?

Steve: Initially, I wanted to become a better fighter. However, when I joined Danny in

Rick: How long did it take after that lesson for you to adapt and start fighting to earn points?

Steve: Well, I started training harder and gained a better understanding of what I

needed to do. So I went back to training, and as I followed the teachings of Danny inasanto, I began to improve. Once I started to improve, I never looked back.

Rick: Were there many black martial artists in martial arts schools back in the '50s and early '60s, or were there very few?

Steve: In my school, it was just me. Everyone there, including those who studied under Dan Inasanto something, could beat me when using karate. I thought, "I don't know about this," but I wasn't going to quit. I decided to continue until I learned. As I improved, someone named Norman Pat suggested I try fighting him in a tournament. I discovered I was quick in my movements, didn't know much, but I could make enough moves to score a point. I began to love the science of fighting and wanted to be the best I could be at that time.

Rick: Did you get to know Jim Kelly during the '60s, before "Enter the Dragon"?
Steve. Yes, it was around 1971 when I heard of him.

Rick: So, you knew him before "Enter the Dragon" was made? You were familiar with him before the movie was released?

Steve: I'm trying to think back. I don't believe I knew him at the time when he was involved in making the movie. I'm trying to recall if I knew him by then or met him later.

Rick: Donnie mentioned that he didn't really like Jim Kelly at the time because he had another school. Did he have a school close to yours, where they filmed "Enter the Dragon"?

Steve: You're referring to Jim he did have a school. Yes, but it was my School they filmed at for "Enter the Dragon," but I do not remember meeting him personally before that.

Rick: How did it come about? What's the most interesting thing for you now that you found yourself in the opening scenes, at very iconic moment when Jim Kelly walks in, and your training the class at the front .After the movie opened up, you saw thousands of schools suddenly appearing from nowhere, and a lot of the youth at that time wanted to be like Jim Kelly or Bruce Lee.

Steve: Well, we had seen Bruce in what they call the Green Hornet. That's what we knew about him.

Rick: Originally, before they cast Jim, were they considering other people like you for that role?

Steve: Yes, I received a phone call about being in a movie called "Enter the Dragon." I knew nothing about it, so they asked if I wanted to be in it, and I said yes. The same night we were shooting the movie, Jim came in. To make it short, when they asked if he was in the Screen Actors Guild, he said yes. When they asked me, I said no. I didn't know anything about the Screen Actors Guild at the time. They tried to postpone it until the next day, but they said no. We need to get this done tonight. So, when he came in, he got that part.

Rick: So, it could have been a different story if you had a Screen Actors Guild card. It could have been you playing that part in "Enter the Dragon," right?

Steve: That is true.

Rick: Do you have any regrets about that?
Steve. Yes, I wish I had the chance again to do something like that.

Rick: Did you ever meet Bruce Lee?

Steve: Oh, yes, Bruce and I were friends.

Rick: So, how did you meet Bruce?

Steve: I was fighting in a tournament one night, and he and Chuck Norris were sitting together. He asked Chuck who I was, and Chuck told him Steve Sanders. So he wanted to come out and meet me. He came out and tapped me on the shoulder right after I had a fight. He said, "You have extremely fast hands and feet," and I thanked him. We sat and talked for a while, and when he was about to leave, he asked if I knew who he

Steve Muhammad

UASE URBAN ACTION SHOWCASE and EXPO

UASE 11

URBANACTIONSHOWCASE.COM

Steve: He became friends with people he liked, and if he disliked someone, he'd let you know. So, he was very sharp in the science of fighting. He didn't perform like he did on TV or in movies, as those movements were specifically for the screen. In real life, he knew those things wouldn't work. But his movements were very impressive, and I found him to be a very skilled fighter, albeit different from what you saw on the movie screen.

Rick: Did you spar with Bruce?

Steve: Oh yes, I did. It was quite an experience.

Rick: What was it like sparring with him? He was fast, right?

Steve: Oh yes, he had what I'd call uncanny timing, which meant his timing could match your speed. From what I saw when he was fighting, he was a very skilled fighter with both hands and feet.

Rick: You became close friends, right? Steve. Yes, we were good friends. We never visited each other's homes, but whenever we met, we were very close and friendly.

Rick: You both had a mutual respect in martial arts, right?

Steve: Yes, we were kindred spirits in martial arts and learned from each other.

Rick: Did you manage to get any photographs with Bruce?

Steve: Oh, he left, I think, after "The Green Hornet." He left and went to Hong Kong. Our friendship, the closeness that we had, it ended there. I do have a letter from him that he sent to me from Hong Kong if I can find it now.

Rick: That would be nice. If you locate it, we can scan it and include it in your article. It adds some historical context to the situation If you find it, great. If not, just let me know. (Sadly he could not find it). Was it because of Bruce Lee that you were considered for your role in the early sequences of "Enter the Dragon"? Or did it happen through a completely different channel? Were they searching for a skilled black martial artist, or did Bruce mention your name during casting?

was. I said no, and he said, "Bruce Lee." I ran towards him and grabbed him because he was our hero at the time. I was jumping up and down, thinking, "Man, I just met Bruce Lee." So, I gave him my phone number. We used to go to his place to work out. There's something people don't know: Bruce could put a dime or a pen in his hand and take it out of your hand. We used to put on a little show and make money. What I did was put three pennies on my hand and threw them in the air, catching them one by one, making it seem like I had incredible timing.

Rick. What were your impressions of Bruce Lee having met him? He obviously, at that stage, nobody had really seen his screen presence and his ability on screen. But I mean, you met him before his fame because the Green Hornet only survived one season. So, you know, The Green Hornet didn't really work like Batman did as a series in the UK. We got the series very late. But how did you find him as a person? He always strikes me, and I've written many books on Bruce Lee, that he was very charismatic and focused. What was your impression of Bruce Lee?

Steve: I can't recall the name of the guy from Robert Clouses office who contacted me about being in "Enter the Dragon." I received a phone call from them, and I agreed to do it. However, as I mentioned earlier, Jim Kelly was already a member of the Screen Actors Guild, and when he found out about the part, he inquired about it. Because I wasn't in the Screen Actors Guild, they gave the part to him.

Rick: What were your impressions of the film when you saw it in the cinema in 1973? Donnie mentioned that he told everyone he was the star and that they should watch for his brief appearance. What did you think of the film? It has stood the test of time, and it's still being reissued in different formats. "Enter the Dragon" remains timeless because it's set on an island, with everyone wearing karate uniforms and no cars, making it not easily dated. It's considered one of the greatest martial arts films. What were your thoughts on "Enter the Dragon"?

Steve: I thought at the time that I had never seen a movie quite like it. It was magnificent. The way they had set it up, compared to the martial arts movies we were used to, was different. The movements in "Enter the Dragon" felt more like actual fighting rather than just putting on a show. We saw it as one of the best martial arts films we had ever watched.

Rick: Did you watch Bruce Lee's other films that he made before "Enter the Dragon," such as "The Big Boss" or "Way of the Dragon"?

Steve: I watched everything he did.

Rick: I'm sure you did. After "Enter the Dragon," it sparked a Kung Fu craze in many places. People began watching all sorts of Kung Fu movies. Did you also enjoy watching other Kung Fu films outside of Bruce Lee's work?

Steve: Before Bruce Lee, we were watching those movies, and after Bruce Lee, we were looking for the same movements that we saw in those movies, which were beautiful. We were expecting that from everyone else who practiced karate, and they started improving after Bruce Lee.

Rick.:Yes, things changed.

Steve: So, I believe he had something that he showed us, which helped us in advancing in the martial arts, especially in movies.

Rick: Well, Bruce Lee movies that were released after it, even though they were filmed before in Asia, became such an influence on so many people, actors, and fighters. He's probably the most influential person who opened up the world of martial arts cinema. I used to say "in the beginning that people flirted with martial arts, but it wasn't until Bruce Lee came along that we fell in love with them" because young kids and adults, wanted to be like Bruce Lee. They wanted to do flying kicks, use nunchucks, and make war cries. You trained with him personally. Did you pick up anything from Bruce? Did he enhance your fighting skills while sparring with him?

Steve: Oh, yes, he did. I was a student under Ed Parker, and he came from a different Chinese style. Although both were Chinese styles, he had a different approach to fighting. I don't want to brag, but I wasn't slow, and I had good movements for both offense and defence. When we sparred with each other, we would often stop and laugh at the unique movements we could use against each other. We'd ask questions like, "How did you do this? How did you do that? What did you see that made you move when you did?" So, I would say we certainly helped each other, and our styles complemented each other.

Rick: I've heard this from people I've interviewed before. I think Bruce Lee was

a bit of a sponge. He liked to learn from others. He wasn't afraid to use what he learned. I've spoken to people like Juan John Lee and Nick, who said that when they trained with him, they learned from each other. Juan, a high-level Taekwondo practitioner, said he tried to help Bruce improve his kicks while Bruce helped him with his hand techniques. I believe that when Bruce asked someone to join him, it's because he saw their worth and believed he could learn from them and adapt their techniques. So, he didn't spar lightly, and if he invited you, it was because he saw something in you that could enhance his abilities, while also improving yours.

Steve: I remember Bruce showing me a film when I was a white belt, and when I saw this guy moving, I thought, and he was moving, and I thought, "Man, his movements are terrible." I was wondering who this person was. Then he brought the film closer, and I said, "Oh, hell, that's me." I didn't even know that he had filmed me when I was a white belt.

Rick: Do you have a copy? Did he film it himself with his own camera while sitting there?

Steve: I'm not sure where he got it from, but on that same film, he had me filmed as a brown belt, and then as a black belt.

Rick: Well, Bruce used to carry a camera. If you look at some of his early footage, he's in the back garden with Dan Inosanto, with James Coburn, and Abdul Kareem Jabbar. He liked to film to study. So if he saw something, it wouldn't surprise me if he had filmed it.

Steve: He might have obtained it from someone else. I'm not certain if he filmed it himself, but he had footage of me as a white belt, brown belt, and black belt. He showed me as a brown belt, and it wasn't clear at first until he brought it into focus. On this one, I said, "Oh, that guy's not bad," not realising it was me. When he brought it up close, I had a big smile on my face. He said, "Now, let's watch the next one." He saw my improvements through the ranks, from white belt to brown belt to black belt. He noticed a specific movement that I introduced. Even today, people who were around at that time will tell you that, instead of being flat-footed when I fought, I raised the heel of my back foot off the floor. This allowed me to move

forward faster and make quicker movements than others in martial arts at the time. Initially, I was taught to fight flat-footed, but as I continued, the traditional stances, like the Kempo stance, became uncomfortable due to my bone structure. I informed Danny Inosanto, and he advised me to change it. I thought to myself, "All this time, I've been struggling with this stance, and all I had to do was change it."

Rick: That's how Bruce was. Bruce was a cha-cha champion. When you saw Bruce fight, it was as if he was dancing. He had a unique fluidity and movement. Many people imitated that, rather than adopting a stiff and rigid stance. Did you follow Bruce's more flexible and free style, or were you a more rigid fighter?

Steve: I knew that. As a black man, I had a certain type of rhythm. I had to find out what that rhythm was. I didn't really find out what the rhythm was until few years back, but I knew that I had to have a rhythm. So if you look at me, fight and some of the old films,

you'll find me shifting and moving around and having trying to develop a rhythm but an offbeat rhythm in fighting and I think that I developed that.

Rick: Well, everybody's got their own rhythm. It's just finding it. You can't really copy people. You just have to find your own beat your own rhythm that works best for you.

Steve: Well, I think that, uh, from what I've learned over the years, every race has a rhythm because you find that all of us have a drum beat. But those drum beats are different. So with those drum beats, they make a rhythm. I would say with black people there's a four count rhythm that we use. And it can be upbeat producing formless rhythm from the rhythm of wisdom. But you have to have wisdom within that rhythm. And once you can do that, you're rhythm for fighting change for the better.

Rick: I mean, you still look in good shape. What's your level of training these days?

Because you still look like you're in. You still look young in the face. I don't. See any stress? Wrinkles or you know nothing like that. So you're doing something right? Maybe you can tell us the secret.

Steve: Thank you I try to live a good clean life and I teach three days a week.

Rick: You know, it's amazing. I've met a couple of people in their 70s who are still in movies. They've lived clean lives, and they look good. They stand straight, and they can still go for it. So, whatever you do, whether its martial arts or anything else, one thing I've noticed is that you must stick with it. It's easy in today's world to wander off in life through various distractions. But those who've remained dedicated seem to have eternal youth and maintain good posture. I think to myself, no matter what your motivation is, it's good to keep at it as long as you can physically manage it. Maybe not at the same level as when you were in your 20s, 30s, or 40s, but for someone like you, who's been at it for so many years, it must be second nature. Do you know what I mean? It must be ingrained in you. Even if you're not as quick or agile as before, you still look great. I'm not even sure how old you are; I didn't check that before this conversation, but your face looks very healthy. When I practiced Tai Chi, we used to do this thing where the teacher would examine someone's face, look at their tongue, and it had a connection to their stomach's condition. He'd say that before he even started teaching, he could look at a person and tell a lot about their health by examining their tongue. Things like blue under your eyes or bags under your eyes could reveal a lot. But when I look at someone like yourself, you appear very clean, like a man in his 20s, with good skin and everything. All power to you, it gives people like me hope.

Steve: Oh, yes, sir. I live by four laws: spiritual law, dietary law, fitness law, and skill law. The spiritual, dietary, and fitness laws are things you must follow every day to stay healthy. I'm 84 years old

Rick: Well I am really looking forward to seeing you "Urban Action Showcase" in New York and talking more about Bruce Lee and thank you for taking time out to talk for me this special edition.

Steve: Thank you Rick look forward to seeing you.

Bishop
Donnie Williams
From Enter The Dragon to Beyond!
Interview By Rick Baker

Rick: Hi, Donnie It's lovely to meet you. I would like to start by getting a some background on your career and your journey into martial arts.

Donnie: Just ask anything you want Rick.

Rick: "Could you please share some insights about your early days and how you initially became involved in karate? I understand you have been practicing it for many years. So, I'm curious to know how you first ventured into martial arts during a time when it wasn't as mainstream as it is today. Could you tell me about your journey, Donny?"

Donnie: "Alright, my introduction to martial arts during my early years was influenced by racial prejudice. I had a strong resentment towards white people, which stemmed from being on the receiving end of violence and discrimination while growing up in Savannah, Georgia until the age of 12. I lived in the heart of the ghetto, faced constant condemnation and lived in an environment rife with challenges. My mother worked for white families who, unfortunately, didn't treat her with fairness or kindness. This further fuelled my personal grievances, leading me to hold negative views based on my own experiences. When we relocated to California when I was 12, racial tensions and conflicts persisted in my life. It was during my time in California that I decided I wouldn't allow another white person to defeat me. This determination led me to venture into martial arts, which I began practicing in the backyard, that's how my journey into martial arts began during my early days."

Rick: What was the first style of karate that you fell in love with? Was it Shotokan Karate, or was it a different style?

Donnie. "It was Shotokan karate system under sensei Jerry Atkins I then joined the military because I aspired to become tough. It was my personal desire to be strong, even though I was a slender young black man.

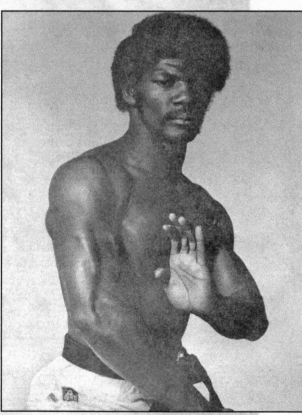

I wanted to toughen up, and that was my motivation."

Rick: How old were you when you took your first lesson?

Donnie: "I was around 16 at the time when I started to take Martial Arts seriously I couldn't afford the Friday lessons. So, I traded me doing some odd jobs for him, and he allowed me to clean the school, and that's where we essentially had our martial arts."

Rick: "Did you find that? I know some people who mention that they have many friends, especially black friends who harken back to the 60s and 50s, and they took up martial arts due to racial issues. But they soon discovered that it was more than just self-defence. They found that they genuinely enjoyed it. They relished the training, and for some, it even held a spiritual aspect. What was your experience with learning it? Was it purely because you wanted to be better at self-defence and standing your ground, or did you eventually discover that it was a discipline you genuinely enjoyed?"

Donnie: "No, it wasn't about 'standing your ground' It was about being the best, I had an attitude. You have to understand; I was a racist and had a racist attitude. I really didn't care about or respect people. To update you, when I entered the military, I really wanted to train badly. During my 13 months and 13 days in Vietnam, there was a group called the Tiger Division. They would wake up at 5:00 every morning and go to the beach area in Penang for their cold training they only wore gis, and they impressed me so much that I wanted to be like them. I eventually found the art of taekwondo with Master Byong Yu, who was the Grandmaster in the San Francisco area. After finding him, I trained with him for about a year and a half. I even lived in his garage and at the karate school. So my early days were all about pursuing excellence and striving to be the best. All of this happened before I met Steve Mohammed."

Rick: "Were you grading for belts, or

were you engaging in sparring? Were you participating in any competitions, or was it purely one-on-one with the trainer?"

Donnie: "Well, I trained to earn a belt, yes, but I did not compete in competitions because I didn't think about it. Remember, I was talking to a different person than I am now. I agree, I was cocky, racist, negative, and all of that. However, I trained to earn a belt, and the reason I wanted the belt was to be the best in the school because the belt determined your position in the school. So, in a year and a half, I went from a green belt to a black belt. I trained every day, all day. I did nothing but Taekwondo every day."

Rick: "Did it become quite an obsession? Were you very focused? Did the training turn into something akin to an addiction, much like Bruce Lee's dedication?"

Donnie: "Absolutely, I was incredibly obsessed with martial arts. I mean, I would even use my foot to press elevator buttons instead of my hand, just to maintain control. I would attempt to kick near a lamp to see if I could get close without hitting it. My obsession with martial arts was intense, and it's essential to remember that during this time, Bruce Lee wasn't the household name he is today. So, I didn't have Bruce Lee to emulate or act like in any way.

Rick: "It's interesting because you began training in the mid-'60s, for most of the people I interview, they were inspired by Bruce Lee. It's fascinating to encounter someone who started training before Bruce Lee, without getting caught up in what I called the "Kung Fu craze". After Bruce Lee's movies hit the cinemas, every school and dojo were flooded with people wanting to be like him. So you were already into it. Did you end up participating in more tournaments after achieving your black belt? Did you start teaching? What was your next step?"

Donnie: "Well, when I earned my black belt from Master Byong Yu, I ended up doing demonstrations. We had expos and demos for colleges and schools, and we travelled all over California at first. Then we expanded to Texas, and we just kept doing it. I was part of the demonstration team called the Expo team." After that I I decided I needed to find a teacher because I felt that I was only a skilful A performer. I really wasn't a fighter, I Just a performer.

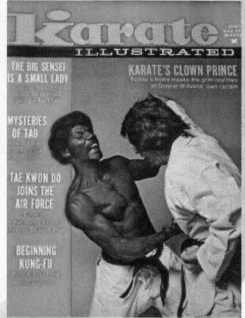

Rick: When you joined a club was there many other Black Fighters in the class.

Donnie: "It was primarily I, along with individuals of Oriental backgrounds, including Japanese and Chinese, but no one of White descent. I can't recall any other Black practitioners at that time. However, when I left Master Byong Yu and moved to Southern California, I went in search of a man named Steve Muhammad, who was associated with Ed Parker. I had heard a lot about this guy, Steve Sanders (Muhammad), who was working with Ed Parker, who, in turn, was training Elvis Presley. So, I figured I had to find this guy, Steve - he must be the one I needed. After some searching, I finally located the place where he was training in Los Angeles. When I got there, I saw some guys training, and I assumed they were his students, but they weren't very impressive. My mind-set at the time was that I believed I was the best, although, in reality, I wasn't. You have to understand my state of mind. I thought I was the best, so I stood up and said these words in a room with about 15 guys, maybe two of them were black belts. I declared, 'You guys are really sorry. I think I can beat anyone in this school, including the teacher,' because I wanted to prove myself.

Then, a 12-year-old boy who was sitting there looked up at me and said, 'Hey, Sir, do you know who this is?' I looked over, and there was a guy, a little skinny guy sitting down nearby. I replied, 'No, and I really don't care.' He said, 'That's Steve Sanders.' I swallowed my gum, looked over at Steve, and realized I had to get out of this big, bold talk. So, I said, 'I and Steve Sanders could take all of you on together.' That made everyone laugh, and my attitude changed because I wanted to meet with Chief Steve and train with him.

I had blown it with my cockiness, and I thought he would never even speak to me after that. I also thought we might get into a fight because I had seen many of his fights in tournaments, and I knew he was fast and highly skilled. He had my respect, even though no one else did."

Rick: "So what happened after that? Did you and Steve become friends, and did he train you?"

Donnie: "Well, after that, I asked him to train with me, and he agreed. I told him about my background and where I was from. He didn't have a formal school, but he trained in the park and at his house. So, we

OUTSIDE U.S.A. $1.25

INSIDE
THE ULTIMATE IN MARTIAL ARTS COVERAGE !
KUNG FU
VOL. 4 NO. 12 FEBRUARY 1978

**CLINT EASTWOOD
RUNS INTO
DONNIE WILLIAMS**

**THE DECEPTIVE HANDS
OF WING CHUN**

**HOW TO PUT ENDURANCE
IN YOUR MUSCLES**

became friends and began training together back in '68. From there, I'll let the rest of the story speak for itself."

Rick: So how did you find yourself, being a part of without doubt the biggest martial arts film "Enter the Dragon "ever to hit are movie screens?

Donnie: Master Byong Yu was training a man by the name of Stirling Silliphant. who was his young student and hehad to go back to Korea. While he was in Korea, Sterling asked me to train and work out with him. Sterling was working with Paul Heller and Fred Weintraub. So, I went to Warner Brothers to work out with Sterling and meet up with Fred Weintraub, Fred Heller, and Paul Weintraub.

It's important to note that I wasn't their friend or anything; I was just there with Sterling. After a period of time, they were working on "The Green Hornet." They were also involved in something related to Harvest, although I'm not entirely sure about the details as they were talking on the telephone.

Rick: So how was the introduction made that saw you getting a role in the movie?

Donnie: Well, they were looking for a karate man, specifically a black karate expert for this role. They wanted to know if I could be provide if they needed, will need to play alongside Bruce Lee. So, I recommended Steve Mohammed. I thought, 'Yeah, I'm going to try help this guy. He's amazing.' At that time, I was working out with Steve, and I knew him personally. I even lived in his home for a couple of years, so we were close friends, not just acquaintances.

Then, Robert Clouse asked me if I could arrange to contact Steve Mohammed. He did reach out to Steve but unfortunately, Steve didn't possess a Screen Actors Guild card at the time. Back then; having a Screen Actors Guild card was a prerequisite. Directors couldn't just cast you unless the role was exceptionally unique and nobody in the Guild could fulfil it."

Rick: Oh I see what a blow for Steve.

Donnie: "So, they couldn't use Mohammed, and Jim Kelly ended up being the choice. The name that Jim Kelly used at the time was Williams.
Donnie. "Oh yeah, I knew Jim Kelly. In fact, I didn't necessarily like him because he had a

school up from our school in Los Angeles, so we were not friends. In fact, his school was in competition with our".

Rick: That reminds me, of the old school Kung Fu Movies (LOL).

Donnie: "Yes, yes, yes. Anyway, after Jim Kelly got the movie, I'm not sure what the right word is, maybe 'as a gesture of gratitude' from Robert Clouse, they said they'd use your school to film a scene. I tell people that Steve and me had significant roles in that movie. I always tell people I've been in 17 films. I even had a co-starring role in a film just two years ago. But 'Enter the Dragon,' in

which I appeared for only 3.2 seconds, is the one I like to mention. I used to jokingly say I was the star of that movie, though I knew it wasn't true. That movie catapulted the Black Belt Division. It launched me and put us in a position to become the leading martial arts trainers at the time"

Rick: Because I imagine that after 'The Dragon' was screened all over the world, and when people saw it, they flocked to clubs to become like Bruce Lee. When you first heard about this film that you were offered a part in, you probably had no idea that it was going to be a success; it was just

going to be another movie."

Donnie: "Exactly, back then, we just wanted to be in a movie, you know. In fact, we didn't think it was going to be that successful because we didn't train for it, and we didn't get a great line to say. I can still remember my line today - it was 'Ready. OK.' I never got paid for that. But back then, I was just glad to be in the movie."

Rick: "So had you heard of the name Bruce Lee, at the time you were offered a part in the movie? Or was that still a name that hadn't really crossed over to the West yet, apart from maybe the Green Hornet? So, had you heard of Bruce Lee back then?"

Donnie: Yeah, I met Bruce before the movie at Warner Brothers.

Rick – tell me more.

Donnie: "At Fred Weintraub's office, where I met him, I mean, when I met him, he wasn't a big star. You know, even the Green Hornet wasn't as popular as it turned out to be later."

Rick: "He had found fame in Hong Kong with 'The Big Boss,' and he was like an Asian superstar, but he wasn't really known in the West as yet."

Donnie: "Exactly, Yes, and so, my intent was to just get in the movie, and Muhammad gave me the break by calling me up. I ended up throwing two punches, my big role in a big movie. I don't even know what that movie made, but it had to have done over 100 million dollars worldwide."

Rick: Well, the movie has somewhere around $700 million worldwide on budget of just $850,000 USD, which today would still make it one of the highest grossing action films ever.

Donnie: Is that right!

Rick: "If you listen to the original early radio plays, they were plugging John Saxon, Jim Kelly, and Bruce Lee was third. That's before it opened. A few days after it opened Bruce Lee is now the top name. as we no Bruce sadly never got to see that film come out. But it certainly generated a fever like no other film had done. You said you met Bruce Lee, did you have a conversation at all when in his company?"

Donnie: Absolutely!

Rick: "I have spoken to a few people that he was a small guy in stature, but he had a charisma that lit up the room; He had a glowing aura around him. When you met him, what impression did he make on you? "Because he could also be a bit cocky to with attitude bit like you as a young man (smile)

Donnie: Yes he was

Rick: "He had the same mentality as you. 'I'm the best. I'm going to beat everybody now.' That was his mentality. Train, train, train. I'm gonna beat everybody. If I can't beat that guy with 20 punches, I'm gonna learn to do a one-inch punch. I want to learn to do something, you know what I mean? Because I don't want to be fighting for 5 minutes, I want it to be over in seconds, not these long fights you see in the Kung Fu films.' And I mean, when that film opened, you must have been quite sad that he passed before seeing the film that catapulted him to a superstar. I mean, when he died, you must have remembered the day he died. You know, I mean, when it was all over the world, such a young guy."

Donnie: It was tragic I had some good memories with him and Chuck Norris. "I don't want to say Chuck was a friend, but he was an acquaintance that I knew very, very well. Chuck Norris lived in the neighbourhood, Rowland Heights, and I would go to Chuck Norris's house. I've never been to Bruce's house. But Chuck told me Bruce lived a couple of blocks from him up in Rowland Heights. So we'd be at Chuck Norris's house, and Bruce would come down. But, you know, again, I don't want it to sound like me and Bruce was buddies, because we weren't, you know. I was just a person in the room."

Rick: What I would have given to have just been a person in the room with Bruce lee in attendance.

Donnie: "But I don't want to make it sound like Bruce and I were buddies' and I hung out with him, and he promised me something. No, I was in the same space that he was in at the same time, and I had the same cockiness that he had, that 'he's blessed to be in my presence' type of attitude."

Rick: "Yeah, I mean, what impact did that

film have on you when you watched it back? Did you attend one of the early screenings? Were you there when it opened up, or did you go to the premiere? What was it like the first time you saw "Enter the Dragon" that film on the big screen back in 1973?

Donnie: "The first time I saw it was at the theatres; I didn't go to the screening. I wasn't invited, so I didn't go to the screening. The first time I saw it was at the theatre, and I had no idea, okay, I had no idea they used a portion of my face on the screen like that. When I popped up, man, you couldn't believe it. I was like, 'I'm ready to sign autographs' because…(Smile)

Rick: So you enjoyed your first 15 minutes of fame"

Donnie: "So, when I saw it, I called all my friends. I told everybody to go see that movie. Well, they thought I was telling them to go see Bruce Lee, but I was telling them to go see those 3.2 seconds that I was there."

Rick: This was a great break for Jim Kelly

Donnie: "Yes, Jim Kelly did a good job. Bruce Lee did a good job. Saxon did. They all did a really good job in this movie. I heard somebody's gonna try. to re-make "Enter the Dragon".

Rick: Lots of Talk but I believe the rights have been acquired "The Rizza" So let us see. Did you have a conversation with Bruce whist you was in the room?

Donnie: "You know, it's like being in the same room with Elvis Presley. I had the opportunity to be in the same room with Bruce Lee. I shook his hand, exchanged a few words with him, but I doubt he would have remembered me later on. Bruce was at Warner Brothers, in Fred's office, and we had a conversation. However, Bruce's English wasn't very strong, and he mostly delivered one-liners. It was challenging to have a full conversation with him. I remember him asking if I would consider starring in another movie and mentioning something about a future project he had in mind. Regrettably, his untimely passing meant that nothing came of it."

Rick: "When you met him, some people have mentioned that when they encountered him, even though he was a relatively small guy, there was this

undeniable charisma surrounding him. Did you e experience that when you met him? Did you feel something special when you saw him?

Donnie: Oh, yes. Oh yeah. Would he walk in the room? You know, he was somebody special. He did not walk in the room shy.

Rick: Did you attend any of his demonstration?

Donnie: Yes, I attended the one he did at Long Beach
Rick. Was that the one Chuck Norris attended?

Donnie: The one with Chuck Norris one, So, I mean, once again, all of this that I'm sharing with you is that as much respect as I have for Bruce, I'm a realist. I know that Bruce was probably the greatest martial artist ever to grace the film industry, during his life, and he was fast when he was doing live demonstrations.

Rick: They have just done another release of "Enter the Dragon" as we celebrated its 50th Anniversary. The film is as popular today as it was when it broke box office records around the world.

Donnie: It's a great movie and timeless, I watch it only a couple of months ago, I am so grateful to have been a part of it, it opened up many doors for me and many other Black martial Artists.

Rick: You can watch yourself in 4K now crystal clear.

Donnie: LOL I sure can.

Rick: I know you will be attending the "Urban Action Showcase 11 2023" So I look forward to chatting more with you when we meet up. And you're going to be on the front cover of this issue.

Donnie: I love it Rick, cannot wait to meet you.

Rick: It's been great chatting to you and looking forward to seeing you on the 11th in New York.

Donnie: Thank you Rick, see you there.

Jim Kelly
From Martial Arts Champion To Cimena Icon

By Simon Pritchard

James Milton "Jim" Kelly, born on May 5, 1946, in Millersburg, Kentucky, is a name that resonates deeply with martial arts enthusiasts and film buffs alike. His meteoric rise from a martial arts champion to a silver screen icon is a testament to his skill, charisma, and ability to break boundaries.

Martial Arts Mastery

Kelly's initial foray into martial arts began with his training in Okinawan karate under the tutelage of instructor Parker Sheldon. Demonstrating a natural affinity for the art, Kelly swiftly made a name for himself in the competitive circuit. His crowning achievement was securing the World Middleweight Karate title at the 1971 Long Beach International Championships.

"Enter the Dragon": A Game Changer

In 1973, the martial arts film world was forever changed with the release of "Enter the Dragon." Produced as a joint venture between Warner Bros. and Golden Harvest, it was the first film to bridge the cinematic styles of the West and the East.

Jim Kelly was cast as "Williams," a character that showcased not only his martial arts prowess but also his distinctive charisma. Kelly's portrayal of Williams was crucial in introducing a strong African-American character in a major martial arts movie. With his iconic afro hairstyle and remarkable fighting sequences, his character quickly became a fan favourite. Beyond the screen, Kelly's role in this film was ground-breaking, setting a precedent for diverse representation in a genre that had been historically limited in its inclusivity.

Life Post "Enter the Dragon"

The immense success of "Enter the Dragon" opened numerous doors for Kelly in Hollywood. He became a leading figure in the "Blaxploitation" film movement of the 1970s. Some of his notable movies include:

Black Belt Jones (1974): A martial arts action film where Kelly played the titular role, showing his versatility as both a martial artist and an actor.

Three the Hard Way (1974): Another classic, it saw Kelly team up with fellow stars Fred Williamson and Jim Brown to prevent a black genocide plotted by white supremacists.

Hot Potato (1976): This action-packed film had Kelly playing a role similar to his previous characters but set against the backdrop of a political rescue mission in Southeast Asia.

Black Samurai (1977): Here, Kelly played Robert Sand, a secret agent skilled in martial arts, on a mission to rescue his girlfriend from warlords.

Throughout the late 70s and early 80s, Kelly continued to appear in movies and made several TV appearances. However, as the 1980s progressed, he began to take on fewer roles, and by the early 1990s, Kelly had mostly retired from acting.

Outside of cinema, Kelly was a passionate tennis player and established himself in the professional tennis circuit during the 1970s.

Legacy and Passing

Jim Kelly's contributions to cinema and martial arts are undeniable. He paved the way for future generations of African-American martial artists and actors, challenging stereotypes and pushing for inclusivity in a genre where it was lacking.

On June 29, 2013, the world lost this icon when Jim Kelly passed away. His legacy, however, remains alive and well in the hearts of fans worldwide, ensuring his place in history as a martial artist, actor, and trailblazer.

Filmography

Melinda (1972) – Charles Atkins
Enter the Dragon (1973) – Williams
Black Belt Jones (1974) – Black Belt Jones
Three the Hard Way (1974) – Mister Keyes
Golden Needles (1974) – Jeff
Take a Hard Ride (1975) – Kashtok
Hot Potato (1976) – Jones
Black Samurai (1977) – Robert Sand
The Tattoo Connection (a.k.a. E yu tou hei sha xing, Black Belt Jones 2) (1978) – Jones
Death Dimension (1978) – Lt. Detective J. Ash
The Amazing Mr. No Legs (a.k.a. Mr. No Legs) (1979)
One Down, Two To Go (1982) – Chuck
Stranglehold (1994)
Ultimatum (1994) – Executive
Macked, Hammered, Slaughtered and Shafted (2004) – Executive #4
Afro Ninja (2009) – Cleavon Washington
Television
Highway To Heaven (1985/1986) (2 episodes) –Reporter

黒帯(くろおび)ドラゴン　カラー作品

ニューヨークの真只中に吹き荒れる〈ドラゴン〉殺法!
ブルース・リー直伝の必殺技をひっさげて
マフィアに挑む一匹竜!

燃えよドラゴンの
ジム・ケリー／グロリア・ヘンドリー
監督●ロバート・クローズ
脚本●オスカー・ウイリアムズ
製作●フレッド・ワイントローブ
ワイントローブ・ベラー・プロ作品

ワーナー・ブラザース映画

Fred Williamson
Blaxploitation Beyond!
The Resounding Influence of Fred Williamson
By Simon Pritchard

Fred is a former American Football player and has been a prominent film and TV star for over the last 55 years. Fred has starred in such cinema classics as "The Legend of Nigger Charley" (1972), "The Inglorious Bastards" (1978), "Black Cobra" (1987), "From Dust Till Dawn" (1996), and "Starsky & Hutch" (2004), and continues to work today.

Introduction

Fred was born in 1938 in Gary, Indiana. Fred attended Froebel High School and later studied at Northwestern University on a Football scholarship. Fred went on to play for the Pittsburgh Steelers. After being switched to defence in one training session, he became so aggressive the coach of the San Francisco 49er's asked him to stop "Hammering" his players, thus his nickname was born.

Fred went on to play 56 games for the Oakland Raiders. Fred's 75-yard fumble return for a touchdown in 1961 is still the fourth longest in Raiders history (as of 2022). Fred moved to the Kansas City Chiefs, who were also a part of the AFL (American Football League). The Kansas City Chiefs were two-time champions when the AFL amalgamated into the NFL (National Football League). The Kansas City Chiefs went on to play Green Bay Packers in the Super Bowl One final where they lost 10-35.

After leaving Football, Fred started as a TV actor and starred in some of the most popular shows of the time; "Ironside" (1968). "Star Trek: Original Series" (1969), "M*A*S*H" (1970), and the sitcom "Julia" where Fred played her love interest from 1970 – 1971. These roles lead to Fred's first Hollywood film where he played the protagonist in the Western "The Legend of Nigger Charley" (1972). In the same year, Fred starred in the film "The Hammer" and guest starred in the cult classic music show "Soul Train". In 1973 Fred starred in "Black Caesar" and its sequel "Hell in Harlem" with Gloria Hendry (Live and Let Die & Black Belt Jones).

These films are neo-noir crime dramas showcasing crime syndicates in New York. This grew Fred's popularity as an actor showing audiences that he can adapt successfully to a variety of characters. Fred starred in the sequel to "The Legend of Nigger Charley", and "The Soul of Nigger Charley" also in 1973 and the trilogy ended in 1975 with "Boss Nigger" which Fred produced and did the screenplay. The success of these films is still prevalent today as people discuss these films alongside other Spaghetti Western classics such as Sergio Leone's "Man with No Name" trilogy. Fred's films have helped structure Hollywood into what we see on the screen today.

Whilst continuing to make successful films, Fred continued with TV appearances starring in "CHiPs" (1979), "The Jamie Foxx Show" (2000) "Knight Rider" (2009), "The Husbands of Hollywood" (2014 – 2016) a surreal and satirical version of "The Real Housewives '; co-created by Kevin Hart and guest stars include Nick Cannon, Nelly, and one of my favourite comedians, J.B. Smoothe (Curb Your Enthusiasm) and more.

Fred's impact has made him a true star from the football field in the 1950s to films and TV in the 21st Century. Now the Man himself, Fred Williamson.

SP: What was it like growing up in Indiana as a child in the 1940s and Post War America?

FW: Growing up in Gary in the 40's and 50's is probably not much different than any Black family at that time, with one exception… I was a badass.

I was known to fight and not back down from anyone, White or Black. Not only was I a badass, I was a smart student with high scores on my tests. Being a badass with brains were two features they had to consider before bringing me some prejudice crap.
In high school I was a track star: 100 yard dash, mile relay and state shot put champ. I was gifted with speed and size. I was scouted for track scholarships by all the colleges. I chose Northwestern and was the first Black to get a full scholarship. I took advantage of this great opportunity to study and graduated with a BA in Architectural Engineering. And, by the way, I still hold the shot put record at Northwestern University.

After my first year at Northwestern, the new head football coach, Ara Parseghian heard about this track star who was a good size to play football but also was fast. He came to me and convinced me to play football by making my scholarship even better. So after four years at Northwestern, I graduated and

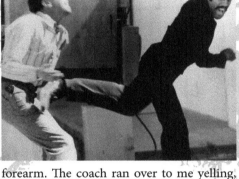

I needed more mental stimulation, and the money we were making then for the whole season was less than players today are making per hour.

So I left football after ten years and started working for Bechtel Steel in San Francisco as an Architectural Engineer. That, however, only lasted nine months because I couldn't make the adjustment to sitting behind a desk at a 9-5 job with one hour for lunch. I started to look for something else.

SP: After football, what made you decide to go into TV & film?

FW: I was watching TV one night and saw a show called "Julia", starring Diahann Carroll. I noticed the guest star each week was a new boyfriend, and I said in my humble way, "I'm better looking than any of these guys." Making a long story short, I moved to LA, got an appointment with the producer and convinced him to hire me for one episode. After that they signed me to be her regular boyfriend on the show. The rest is history.

SP: For people of my generation, especially as a non-American, it is difficult to comprehend what it must have been like to have lived through the pre and post-Civil Rights era. What was it like to get into Hollywood during this time?

FW: I never concern myself about what damn era I'm in. I do my thing my way and move on, over or through any bullshit obstacles. Hollywood likes money so I showed them how to make money with me I decided to make a movie that would raise eyebrows... "Nigger Charley". I knew that would get their attention, and once it hit the theatres it was too late. What this film really showed is that the studios had been missing the Black market. They didn't think a Black could be the star of the film, they usually killed them in the first 5 minutes of the show. I have never nor will I ever do that.

SP: At the start of your career, not only were you called the "N-Word" , it was put in the titles of your films. Although it seems that you have taken this word and re-represented it in a more positive manner in the name of your film "Boss Nigger" (1975). Was this a conscious decision? How do you feel about the use of this word?

FW: My film, "Boss Nigger", was a satire to show how stupid prejudice really is. The word

was signed by the 49ers.

SP: By the late 1950's you had established yourself as a professional Football player; what exactly did you do to earn the nickname "The Hammer"?

FW: On my first day at camp, Coach Red Hickey saw my size and moved me to play Defensive Back. I always played Offense, I had no experience to cover receivers and I looked like I never played the game before.

It wasn't long before the coach came to me and told me if I didn't do better he was going to cut me. What? Cut me and I'd go back to Gary? No way!!! So I had a serious talk with myself that night. I decided I was going to mow all the receivers down at the line of scrimmage. The next day, as a defensive back, I lined up one yard off the receiver, who just happened to be R.C. Owens, an All-Pro Receiver. The coach started yelling at me to get back, but I refused.

They started the play, R.C. Owens took one step off the line and I chopped him with a forearm. The coach ran over to me yelling, "what the hell are you doing?" I said, "I covered him." He stared at me for a moment, then smiled and walked away. Next, he sent a big tight end for me to cover. No problem. These guys had never had a defensive back as big as them and who was also faster.

While I stopped the tight end he didn't go down, but he wanted to fight. So we were trading blows when the coach came over mad at the tight end. Then he looked at me and said, "stop hammering my players so we can get some passing done." At that moment I became "The Hammer".

SP: Football was in its infancy when you played, what do you think of the evolution of the sport from the grassroots to the major industry it is today?

FW: Football is a very physical sport and a good outlet for frustrations. The problem is there can be injuries in football that are hard to overcome. It's physical without apologies. It eventually became boring to me because

BRUTAL!.. BLASTING!.. BLAZING!

FRED WILLIAMSON
IS
Mean Johnny Barrows

MEAN JOHNNY BARROWS starring FRED WILLIAMSON · RODDY McDOWELL
STUART WHITMAN · LUTHER ADLER · JENNY SHERMAN and Special Guest Star ELLIOT GOULD
Produced by and Directed by FRED WILLIAMSON

AN ATLAS FILMS RELEASE

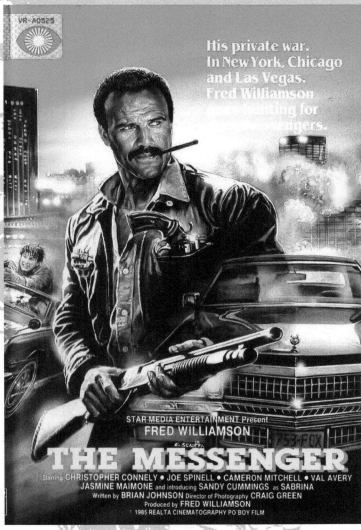

His private war.
In New York, Chicago
and Las Vegas.
Fred Williamson
is hunting for
messengers.

STAR MEDIA ENTERTAINMENT Present
FRED WILLIAMSON
THE MESSENGER
Starring CHRISTOPHER CONNELY · JOE SPINELL · CAMERON MITCHELL · VAL AVERY
JASMINE MAIMONE and introducing SANDY CUMMINGS as SABRINA
Written by BRIAN JOHNSON Director of Photography CRAIG GREEN
Produced by FRED WILLIAMSON
1985 REALTA CINEMATOGRAPHY PO BOY FILM

"nigger" is only a word, it means nothing to me, but obviously means more to other people. Are you trying to say something negative about me? There are more negative words… you are ugly, you stink, etc. Calling me a nigger says nothing negative about me. But if you're saying it to challenge me, then prepare to get your ass kicked. You see the word itself means nothing unless you explain what you are really trying to say.

SP: I have not used the phrase "Blaxploitation films" as I heard that you think it discredits your films. As one of the most famous actors of this 'genre', why do you feel this?

FW: Blaxploitation, what does it really mean? Nothing. Who is being exploited? Black actors are working, they're making more money, and the Black audience is happy to see more Blacks on the screen.

The term was created by the studios to bring these films down. Black films were taking profits away from the high-budget studio films, and they needed this term as

an excuse as to why that was happening. "Nigger Charley" was a $2 million budget, but it outgrossed many big budget major films at that time. Defaming the Black films didn't work and finally Hollywood jumped on the bandwagon. But their interest only lasted about five years.

SP: From Westerns in the early 1970s, you then made a name for yourself in action thriller films. You worked with some of the other greatest actors such as Pam Grier, Jim Brown, Jim Kelly, Gloria Hendry, Richard Roundtree, and Isaac Hayes to name a few, what memories do you have about this time?

FW: It's true the I've worked with other stars, but let me be clear that all the stars you mentioned (with the exception of Isaac Hayes) have worked for me in my productions. My goal was always to control what I do as a producer/director and actor.

My rules in Hollywood: I have to win all my fights and you can't kill me in a movie.

SP: In October 1973 you were the first black man to be the centrefold in Playgirl. What made you decide to do this?

FW: Playgirl was fun and it was more about what I wouldn't show! So ain't much more to say about that.

SP: After the success of writing, co-producing and starring in your own film, you set up Po' Boy Productions in 1975. What made you take the risk and set up your own company?

FW: Setting up my own production company wasn't a risk. I knew how to do everything because I made sure to watch, learn and ask questions about all phases of filmmaking during the first few movies I was in. All I had to do was make sure the characters I played were true to the way they audience saw me. In order to do that, I needed to make my own films.

SP: Between America and Italy you made a lot of films including:

45

- Mean Johnny Barrows (1975)
- Adiós Amigo (1975)
- Joshua (1976) - starred Fred and was directed by Larry G. Spangler who also directed and produced "The Soul of Nigger Charlie" (1973).
- Death Journey (1976)
- No Way Back (1976)
- Mr Mean (1977)

What do you remember about this time?

FW: I soon learned that I was more popular in Europe than in the U.S. Why? Because in America I'm a Black actor, in Europe I'm an action star. My films are now over 70 so you have missed a few!

SP: During the early 1980's you worked a lot with the director Enzo G. Castellari ("The Inglorious Bastards") making post-apocalyptic action thrillers. What was your favourite film you made together?

FW: Working with Enzo Castellari was a complete joy. He understands what directors should do, giving freedom to the actors. That why you chose those actors. Any film with Enzo will be the bes

SP: In 1984 you starred in Warriors of the Year 2072 directed by Lucio Fulci. Lucio, "The Poet of the Macabre", is one of the best and most respected horror directors ever; his films include, "The Gates of Hell Trilogy", "Don't Torture a Duckling", "Zombi 2." What do you remember about Lucio and what was it like working with him?

FW: Working in any foreign film is a great pleasure and always will be. The freedom to act and invent new things is so much better than acting with American directors. Fulci was definitely this type of director. He has the same philosophy as Enzo, you hire the actor you want and then let him act.

SP: From the 1980s to the mid-1990s you starred in action films, the most notable being the cult classic "Black Cobra" which had three sequels. Interestingly "Black Cobra 4 (Detective Malone)" was directed by Umberto Lenzi, the man who created the Cannibal subgenre (Eaten Alive!, Cannibal Ferox). Whilst Italian cinema is internationally recognised and creates what some consider 'masterpieces', why do you think that foreign cinema is not as popular with the general public?

FW: I think American is waking up to foreign production. America spends multi-millions of dollars to produce a film while foreign films bring the same message and pleasure for much less money. Americans equate a masterpiece by their budget, not by the entertainment value. Look at the western genre, the Italian "spaghetti western" is much more entertaining than most American-made westerns, and made for much less money. But it's slowly changing.

SP: In 1994 you appeared in the video which is arguably one of the most famous hip hop songs ever written, "Doggy Dogg World" by Snoop Dogg. The video is made in the vein of a movie teaser. You get out of the car and walk to the club like 'The Don', then a couple of shots later Dr Dre is chillin' with Pam Grier. Do you have any stories for us?

FW: Any stories about Snoop or Dre would put us all in jail - maybe. My best memories are what I have accomplished in my life.

SP: "From Dusk Till Dawn" was written by Quentin Tarantino and directed by Robert Rodriguez. You starred as "Frost", a protagonist at the 'Titty Twister'. This film was crazy and went from a road movie to horror, what was it like working with Quentin and Robert?

FW: He film "From Dusk Till Dawn" was given to me by Quentin and he asked if I would read for him and George Clooney. I gave it some thought and said okay. I gave my interpretation of what he had written, which was different than what he had envisioned. They were both very pleased, but my "no dying" rule had to be kept in place.

By my being bitten and becoming one of the vampires, I would go out as a vampire and a badass badder than me will be the one taking me out!

SP: You are still busy and making films today, is there anything you are working on that you can tell us about?

FW: My latest film is "VFW" Veterans of Foreign Wars. It's streaming now.

SP: Thank you, it has been an honour to be able to speak with a true legend and thank you on behalf of Eastern Heroes. Lastly, is there anything else you would like to add?

FW: The Hammer Ain't Done Yet!

Enter the DRAGON at 50

A Retrospective on Martial Arts Cinema's Pinnacle

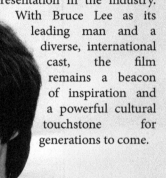

Fifty years ago, on August 19, 1973, "Enter the Dragon" burst onto the silver screen and changed the course of martial arts cinema forever. Directed by Robert Clouse and starring the iconic Bruce Lee, this film was a ground breaking masterpiece that celebrated its 50th anniversary in 2023. "Enter the Dragon" left an indelible mark on the world of cinema, and it continues to influence countless filmmakers and martial artists to this day. With its multi-racial cast, the movie challenged norms and pushed the boundaries of representation in the industry, making it a cultural touchstone for generations.

The Bruce Lee Phenomenon:

At the heart of "Enter the Dragon" is Bruce Lee, the charismatic and incomparable martial artist who transcended racial and cultural boundaries. Bruce Lee's presence as the leading man and martial arts maestro marked a significant milestone in Hollywood's history. As an Asian actor and martial artist, he broke through barriers that were previously insurmountable for actors of Asian descent.

Bruce Lee's philosophy of martial arts and life is beautifully portrayed throughout the film. His character, Lee, exudes wisdom and charisma, and his martial prowess on-screen is nothing short of astonishing. Lee's performance wasn't just about physical prowess but also about breaking stereotypes and promoting the idea that martial arts could be a path to self-improvement and self-empowerment. His character and the film itself helped bridge cultural divides, becoming an inspiration for countless people worldwide.

A Multiracial Cast and Thematic Depth:

"Enter the Dragon" was a pioneer in promoting diversity and inclusion in film. It featured a diverse cast of characters from various racial backgrounds. This multicultural ensemble was virtually unheard of at the time. The film showcased an international martial arts tournament on a remote island, where fighters from different parts of the world converged to compete, highlighting unity in diversity. Beyond the physicality and action, the film delved into deeper themes. It explored the dynamics of power, corruption, and justice. The plot revolves around the mission to expose a powerful crime lord, Han, who uses his martial arts tournament as a front for his illegal activities. The film's thematic depth gave it a resonance beyond the martial arts genre, touching on issues that continue to be relevant today.

Influence on Martial Arts Cinema:

"Enter the Dragon" set new standards for martial arts choreography and fight scenes. The impeccable fight sequences, choreographed by Bruce Lee himself, remain iconic and have been imitated and revered for decades. The film's influence extended far beyond its time, shaping the martial arts genre and inspiring countless future martial arts actors and directors.

The Legacy:

The 50th anniversary of "Enter the Dragon" reminds us of its enduring legacy. It's not just a classic martial arts film; it's a cultural touchstone that stands as a testament to the power of representation and the impact of Bruce Lee. The film opened doors for Asian actors in Hollywood, inspired generations of martial artists, and continues to captivate audiences with its blend of action, philosophy, and cultural significance.

In conclusion, "Enter the Dragon" celebrated its 50th anniversary as a cinematic masterpiece that changed the course of martial arts cinema and pushed boundaries of representation in the industry. With Bruce Lee as its leading man and a diverse, international cast, the film remains a beacon of inspiration and a powerful cultural touchstone for generations to come.

Karen Campbell
A Tale of Resilience and Mastery

Introduction & Biography

Born on 30th September 1963 in a quaint North Welsh town, my life story is a testament to resilience, passion, and perseverance. Tragically abandoned with my younger brother at the tender age of 2, we found solace and care under the loving wings of our grandmother. Despite her already having a full house, she provided us with a life, albeit simple and without extravagance, that was nonetheless filled with happiness.

Education became my sanctuary. Early on, my prowess in sports became evident. At 9, I defied norms as the first female on a male football team. By the time I was 11, my high school recognized my athletic gifts, enabling me to represent our country at the junior level in running and hurdling. I also played hockey and netball for Wales. An invitation for a scholarship at the renowned Ballet Rambert in London came when I was 16. Unfortunately, circumstances didn't permit this dream to be fulfilled.

After a brief stint in karate, where an unfortunate accident set me back, I transitioned into motherhood. Relationships, transitions, and challenges

shaped my journey, but my passion never waned. In Australia, I honed my skills in drama, securing the prestigious Dux award and performing professionally in the 'King & I'. However, life led me back to the UK and into the world of martial arts.

In 1993, a casual conversation about kickboxing set me on a path of unmatched determination. By October that year, I was graded. Training hard and fighting harder, I retained an unbeaten record in the ring. Despite personal upheavals, martial arts and acting became my anchors.

By 2000, I achieved my Black belt, eventually inheriting the club and introducing numerous women to the martial arts world. My martial arts journey intertwined with Shotokan Karate, where I was greatly influenced by Sensei Peter Sheridan, embodying the principles of Honesty, Respect, Loyalty, Sincerity, Spirit, and Perseverance.

Recently, I have channelled my skills and experiences into empowering women, particularly young girls transitioning into new phases of life, teaching them awareness and self-defence.

My service has always been selfless, evident in my volunteer work with children's charities, as a Fire Cadet instructor, and even at Buckingham Palace celebrating King Charles 3rd's 70th birthday. Martial arts are interwoven into my life's fabric. My accolades include being inducted four times into the UK Martial Arts Hall of Fame, the International Hall of Fame India, and the American Hall of Honours. I'm proud to be featured among 200 Inspirational Women in Martial Arts and have the privilege of friendships with renowned figures like Kenny Herrera, and Cynthia Rothrock.

Now at 60, with my 5th Dan black belt awarded in January 2022, my journey remains ever exciting. Every experience,

every challenge, and every accomplishment are threads in the tapestry of my life. And I believe the adventure is far from over.

Cynthia Rothrock and Karen Campbell interview - 5th May 2023. Doncaster Martial Arts Show

Karen: How did you get into movies?

Cynthia: I was in a team with Ernie Reyes Snr, probably a lot of you know who. He is. He's coming to Los Angeles to look for a new they wanted, new "Bruce Lee". They called the West Coast team because the guys on it were phenomenal and he said "shall I bring the girls?" And they said, "yeah, you could bring them down but they're really looking for a guy."

When we went down, I did some form. I did self-defence, I did fighting and I did hook swords and Corey Yuen and says "I

TWIN dRAGONS

want the girl! I want to set the girl up.". It was kind of like, I've never really thought, I'm going to go do movies. It was something that kind of fell in my lap. I thought my first movie would just be another crazy thing I've done in my life. I was thinking that maybe

I'd get on a poster or something and it's something I can show my daughter someday. I didn't really know. I thought it was going to be a onetime thing and that movie was quite successful, and then I got a contract with Golden Harvest for three movies.

Karen: Wow, you definitely are not a onetime wonder, that's for sure. That was in the 80's wasn't it?

Cynthia: Yes, it was. 1985.

Karen: 1985, wow, well, for those who remember that....

Cynthia: Yeah, but here's the good thing. All those Hong Kong movies are now being regenerated into Blu-rays, and they're all coming out now, because there's a company [Eureka] from the UK that is doing them and I have done some interviews with them. The back stories of what went on in those movies. If they're not out there, they will all be coming out.

Karen: Which martial art movies did you enjoy acting in the most?

Cynthia: I have to say that I enjoyed the most was either "Writing Wrongs" or maybe "Lady Reporter", Hong Kong films. I think that the Hong Kong choreographers, and the way they do things over there are brilliant. As far as American movies? "Sworn to Justice".

Karen: And when did that come out?

Cynthia: "Sworn to Justice" came out in 1998.

Karen: Can you tell us who your favourite person to act with is?

Cynthia: That's hard. Everybody that I've acted with, I always become friends with them after. I've done probably about ten movies with Richard Norton and I've done about six with Don Wilson.
This year I'm doing my own movie called "Black Creek" and both Richard and Don are in it and a whole great cast of other people.

Karen: What is your film called and what is it about?

Cynthia: it's called "Black Creek" and we did a crowd fundraiser on Kickstarter and all my friends told me "Don't do it", they said "Michael J. White did it and his he wasn't successful. So, why do you think you'll be successful? Because he's got like 5 million followers." So, i was a little anxious to do it but i put faith in to myself and into my project. We have become the second most successful action picture to ever be funded by Kickstarter.
It's called "Black Creek" and it's a Western and what I'm bringing to the screen is something a little bit different. It's a western with martial art action. It takes place in the 1900s. It's a very dark movie, it's gritty. There's nothing funny about it and it's because I like

Westerns and I love martial arts action, so that's in it. We're shooting it at the end of October.

Karen: I wish you all the success with that and so everybody else says China O'Brien was your first blockbuster. Anything to say about that?

Cynthia: You know China O'Brien was such a popular movie worldwide, and I think it was because many people really haven't seen a woman especially a Caucasian woman, who knows how to fight.
So we have been trying to get the rights to China O'Brien 3 but the company that owns them, they don't want anything to do with it. That is something we'd really love to do, a modern day China O'Brien. What has happened to her, and where she is today.

Karen: So what do you think about the UK? What's what's the best bit about the UK?

Cynthia: I love being here and as a native person, i love being up in the North especially, as it has a lot of scenery. I love the theatre and London has the best theatre and the shopping, and of course, I like the people.

Karen: Could everybody give the biggest thank you and applause to Cynthia Rothrock, Lady Dragon, herself! Thank you.

ENTER THE DRAGON
SHOWCASE SEQUENCE
The Final battle before the showdown

"In the heart-pounding crescendo of 'Enter the Dragon,' we take you on a journey through a series of captivating snapshots, capturing the electrifying battle that precedes the ultimate showdown with the enigmatic and formidable villain, Han. Step into the world of martial arts mastery as we delve into the intense fight sequences that set the stage for the epic clash between Bruce Lee and the nefarious Han. The gallery, aptly titled 'The Battle before The Showdown with Han,' offers a glimpse into the thrilling moments that will leave you on the edge of your seat, eager to witness the martial arts spectacle that lies ahead."

71

Printed in the USA
CPSIA information can be obtained
at www.ICGtesting.com
LVHW060156200124
769097LV00017B/304